ENDING VIOLENCE
in Teen Dating Relationships

AL MILES

A Resource Guide for Parents and Pastors

Augsburg Books
MINNEAPOLIS

I dedicate this book to my wife, Kathy. Since the days of our youth, she has challenged me to be the man God has always intended. Her encouragement, love, patience, and support these past thirty-four years is helping me become that man.

ENDING VIOLENCE IN TEEN DATING RELATIONSHIPS
A Resource Guide for Parents and Pastors

Large-quantity purchases or custom editions of this book are available at a discount from the publisher. For more information, contact the sales department at Augsburg Fortress, Publishers, 1-800-328-4648, or write to: Sales Director, Augsburg Fortress, Publishers, P. O. Box 1209, Minneapolis, MN 55440-1209.

ISBN 0-8066-5131-8

Cover and book design by Michelle L. N. Cook
Cover photo © Antonio Mo/Taxi/Getty Images. Used by permission.
Author photo © Kathy Miles.

The paper used in this publication meets the minimum requirements of American National Standard for Information Sciences—Permanence of Paper for Printed Library Materials, ANSI Z329.48-1984. ♾™

Manufactured in the U.S.A.

09   08   07   06   05   1   2   3   4   5   6   7   8   9   10

Contents

Foreword
by Dr. Jill Murray

As men and women of faith, how many times have you looked at the often dismal conditions in which our youth are living and thought to yourself, "At least they have their Christianity. Thank God they have a moral compass to guide them." By and large, you are absolutely correct: Faith and Christian values can be a great comfort and help to teens in a society that is often openly hostile to spiritual beliefs.

In a perfect world, a teen's lifelong faith would be all that he or she would need to navigate the sometimes dangerous waters of adolescence. Unfortunately, teens today are living in times that are crushingly different than those in which you and I grew up, and a teen's faith may not only be sharply tested, but used against him or her in an abusive relationship.

Does that idea seem incomprehensible? In my experience as a psychotherapist who specializes in abusive teenage dating relationships, as well as an author of three books on the subject, I can tell you that I was as surprised as you may be. I had always thought that "good Christian" boys and girls had the moral fortitude to withstand abuse and certainly couldn't possibly be abusive themselves. How wrong I was! *I have found, in fact, that the vast majority of teenagers I treat for abusive relationships come from Christian homes in which the family attends church every Sunday and are moderately to highly involved in their house of worship.*

In lecturing at conferences around the United States—often sponsored by religious organizations or agencies—I have had the opportunity to speak with hundreds of thousands of middle and high school students, very often at parochial schools. I have lectured at church-based schools in Abilene, Texas; Knoxville, Tennessee; Milwaukee, Wisconsin; and everywhere in between. I find the same results at each school: The teens attending parochial schools experience at least as much abuse in their dating relationships as do their peers in secular schools. These teens appear to be particularly grateful for the information I give them about warning signs of abuse, how an abuser thinks and responds, the emotional roller-coaster the recipient of abuse may be experiencing, how to leave an abusive relationship safely, and how to help a friend in an abusive relationship. When I discuss the ways in which an abuser uses religion as a weapon of abuse, a hush of understanding usually falls over the crowd.

Fortunately for all of us, my good friend, the Reverend Al Miles, understands the dynamic of teenage abusive relationships far better than any clergy member I know, and better than most therapists as well. Rev. Miles and I met several years ago when we were asked to speak at a conference offered on a regular basis for members of the clergy in order to help them understand domestic violence and the ways in which they could be of aid to members of their congregation. I was immediately struck with the thorough understanding of the subject that Rev. Miles has, his passion, and most importantly, his lack of artifice. He did not allow clergy members to shirk behind their title and certainly did not allow them to say, "This sort of thing doesn't happen in my congregation." He told them the way it was and didn't mince his words: "You are foolish if you think that domestic violence has not touched your congregation or that your teenagers are immune to this problem." It was a marvel to watch Rev. Miles draw out these clergy members with wisdom and compassion.

Since that time, he and I have lectured at this same conference each year, and I am amazed every time, learning new ideas from his example. I have read his books, which have made me a better therapist, and I freely recommend them to both parents of faith and to those who struggle with the idea that families of faith experience domestic violence. While his words come from a faith-based philosophy, they are wise beyond any particular religion. Everyone can learn powerful lessons from Rev. Miles.

Our teens are living in a media world that has created distrust, a laissez-faire attitude about sex, a culture in which violence and disrespect run rampant, and a place where women are demeaned at every turn. The media portrays men—especially fathers—as accessories rather than necessities in a child's life and are portrayed as either gangsters or buffoons.

One only has to spend a few minutes watching MTV to understand these points. Listening to the lyrics of popular songs is enough to make a sane person ill. My "favorite" is one in which the chorus sings, "Bitch, you know I love ya, but now I gotta kill ya; Bitch, you know I love ya, but now you gotta die." Make no mistake about it: Both boys and girls watch this with equal unconcern that there is anything wrong with these horrifying songs. The fact that there is so much simulated sex on the videos or that young women are purposely viewed as sluts and whores only adds to the teen male's excitement. Wow, they think, what a terrific life; if only I could have their life! Guns, prostitutes, stolen cars, drugs, sex with as many anonymous people as I can handle; it's all so glamorous! There is no concept of respect for one's own body and mind, much less anyone else's.

Bear in mind that the average teen watches or listens to these kinds of lyrics five to six hours each day and may spend a few more hours instant messaging friends on the family home computer (while pretending to do homework), with messages that are highly sexual and graphic in content.

Editors from teen magazines frequently ask me to give interviews for teen magazines on the subject of teen dating abuse. I recently observed a headline on one of those magazine's covers: "68 Guys You're Going to Want to Sleep With!" It's pretty difficult to compete with the media, isn't it? How many hours each day or week do the teens in your congregation spend in church? Are the messages you are giving teens as compelling as those they watch on TV or read in magazines? It is not enough to tell teenagers, "Don't have sex until you're married" without taking the discussion further. This is similar to telling kids, "Just say no to drugs." They want to know why not and what's in it for them. Thinking that a Christian teen does not have the same hormones as non-Christian teens or that thoughts of sex, substance use, suicide, difficulties with peers, family problems, issues of identity, or concerns about their future do not haunt them is just foolhardy thinking. Believing that being Christian somehow inoculates the young people in your congregation from the pressures of the outside world is not true.

Some of the most common complaints I receive from Christian youth are these:

- I can't talk to my parents; they would never understand. They are so Christian that they don't even know what's going on in the real world.
- My parents think that if I just pray about this problem it will go away.
- I would never think of talking with my pastor. First of all, he would never get it, and second of all, he would tell my parents.

- Sure, I attend youth group, but my youth pastor isn't someone I can talk to about relationships. She pretends like she's all cool and everything, but bring up hooking up and I can tell that she shuts down.
- I want to follow God's laws for me. I know they are good and right but no one has really explained how they work for teenagers. I mean, what am I supposed to do when a guy puts his hands up my shirt? Do I say, "Uh no, God wouldn't want me to do this"? How lame is that?
- My parents want me to only be friends with other Christians and they certainly want me to only date other Christians. I'm only fifteen; it's not like I'm going to marry anyone I date right now, but they are so closed-minded.
- Does the Bible really say that women are supposed to be subservient to men? Does that mean that if a guy tells me to do something, I have to do it? What about my opinion? My boyfriend tells me that women are supposed to be subservient to men all the time and I don't know what to do.
- My parents fight all the time, but then they go to church on Sunday and want me to go with them. I feel like they are hypocrites and just want to look good in front of their friends at church, but you can't believe what goes on in my home. And then they have the nerve to tell me who to date.
- Everyone's having oral sex. It's not really sex, so I'm saving myself for marriage and following God's plan for me.
- A lot of what's in the Bible is old-fashioned and I don't see how it applies to me anyway.

I could go on and on, but I think you get the idea. The teens in your congregation and in your home are crying out for direction and spiritual guidance that they can relate to. More than ever, you are up against formidable foes in terms of the media and a society that doesn't value or respect spiritual beliefs or the family structure.

I am so grateful that Rev. Miles has written this important book and that you have chosen to read it. His breadth of knowledge—both in a religious and secular sense—will astound you as it has me. His tell-it-like-it-is, no-holds-barred approach may catch you off-guard and will certainly make you think about how you can approach the teens in your life. I encourage you to take your time in reading this vital work and to use the techniques he advises. When you complete the book, pass it on to a friend.

Rev. Al Miles is a blessing and a gift to our entire community. I wish both you and him the very best in helping our teens become happier, more responsible adults.

Dr. Jill Murray
Licensed psychotherapist, author, and presenter

Acknowledgments

A book project such as this requires a team of dedicated individuals willing to share their experience, expertise, and time. I thank Jesus Christ for all of the adolescents and adults who chose to take part. I also thank Christ for his guidance and love, which kept me focused and somewhat patient throughout the two years it took to research and write this volume.

The love, respect, and support given to me by my wife, Kathy, throughout the project and our thirty-four-year relationship, took a major role in helping me to shape those sections of the book that deal with healthy dating relationships. I also thank Kathy for typing every page of the manuscript, offering constructive feedback, and for giving me the freedom to spend our already limited personal time completing this work.

Appreciation must also be extended to the staff of Augsburg Fortress, Publishers, for giving me the opportunity to publish with their wonderful organization. Special thanks goes to Michelle L. N. Cook, assistant managing editor at Augsburg Books, for her many insights and production design. The same gratitude is extended to Victoria A. Rebeck, my long-time personal editor. As has always been the case, her expertise with phrases and words helped bring clarity to my thoughts.

Many other people made this book a reality. They read the manuscript, offered insightful comments, provided research material, and suggested people to be interviewed. A big *mahalo* goes to Leah Aldridge, the staff of Alternatives to Domestic Violence, Grace Alvaro Caligtan, Barbara Chandler, Jeffery Chandler, Niki Christiansen, Nelda Rhoades Clarke, Diana Davids, Curtiss Paul DeYoung, Karen DeYoung, Rachel DeYoung, the staff of Domestic Violence Clearinghouse and Legal Hotline, Jordan Goettsche, Akijuwon Greene, Lisa Brito Greene, L. Kevin Hamberger, the staff of Institute on Domestic Violence in the African American Community, Samuel Irons, Jason Kimura, Julie Mall, Shari Miller, Suzan Morrissette, Jill Murray, K. Daniel O'Leary, Gina Graham Palmer, Roy Prigge, Robin R. Runge, Christina Ryder, Vanessa Silver, Carolyn Staats, Chris Stumpff, Mona Takara, Sandra Talavera, Kim Taylor, Stephanie Thomson-Dick, Carol Miles Underwood, Candice Walker, Erica Staab Westmoreland, Oliver Williams, and Amy Woods.

Last, I want to especially thank Amy, "Angie," and "Sarah" for sharing their sacred stories with us. *Mahalo nui loa* for their courage and trust.

Introduction: What Christian Youth Have Taught Me

"Bitch is a female dog. He tells me he loves dogs. So when he calls me his bitch, that must mean he loves me." This was the response from a sixteen-year-old female at a teen-dating violence awareness session I once led for forty adolescents, ages sixteen through eighteen. I had just challenged the group to never call any human being a bitch, and to not allow anyone to describe them with this term because, I said, "bitch" is both degrading and offensive—especially when used to refer to a girl or woman.

This sixteen-year-old female's explanation of why her boyfriend called her a bitch raises several critical questions. Why would any male harbor such disrespect and hatred toward females that he'd have a need to dehumanize them? How did he come to develop such a poor self-image or such a sense of entitlement? Where did he learn that it's okay to call a girl a bitch—the media, his father, friends, school, society? Who beat him down or failed to lift him up? What hope does he have of ever being involved in a healthy dating relationship with any female when misogyny (women-hating) rules his heart and soul?

And what about the feelings and thoughts of the sixteen-year-old female herself: Why would she think it's okay to allow anyone to compare her to a dog? Who's to blame for her acceptance of such denigration? Did she receive positive messages about her self worth from parents, pastors, teachers, and society? Or was she taught to assume a submissive role toward males? What are her chances of ever reaping the benefits of a healthy dating relationship with any male if she continues to live in the subjugated life in which she was placed by society, media, parents, and church?

This sixteen-year-old female was the first, but certainly not the last, youth at that particular dating violence awareness session to disagree with my categorization of "bitch" as a dehumanizing term for girls and women. More than half of the teens in attendance, seven of them females, told me "bitch" was "no big deal." As one of the males claimed, "Our generation uses the word 'bitch,' Rev. Miles, like your generation used terms such as 'honey' and 'sweetie.' No one gets upset."

Some youth at the session, males and females alike, demonstrated that this assertion is false. They called the word "bitch" cruel, degrading, objectifying, offensive, and ugly. One of the females who found the term offensive asked those teens who said they found the term acceptable, "Would it be okay for some guy to call your mother or grandmother a bitch?" Those teens that had defended the term suddenly became very upset. Initially, they even refused to respond to the question posed by their peer. But when she pressed them for an answer, all the teens who had described the term "bitch" as "no big deal" admitted it would not be acceptable for a man to refer to their own mothers and grandmothers in this manner.

Like most of the sessions I conduct on teen dating violence awareness, this one was attended primarily by Christian youth. This particular group of forty consisted of African American, Hispanic, and white adolescents. This brings to mind answers to three frequently asked questions about dating violence among teens. Yes, the problem exists in all ethnic, racial, and socioeconomic groups. Yes, it happens to youth in rural, urban, and suburban areas. Yes, Christian as well as non-Christian youth are both the abusers and abused in these situations. Many Christian parents and pastors are shocked by the latter statement. Somehow, they believe that teen dating violence is only a secular problem. Why would Christian youth be less vulnerable to this issue? They are being raised under the same cultural influences as are non-Christian youth.

Christian teens have taught me an enormous amount about their lives in and outside of dating relationships. The past five years (the last two of which I spent researching and writing this volume), they have given me their trust by speaking candidly about topics such as alcohol and drug use, hip-hop, peer pressure, pop culture, self-esteem, sexuality, and spirituality. Whatever the subject matter, two main themes have emerged from these conversations.

First, teens say they want adults, especially their parents and Christian leaders, to listen to what they are feeling and thinking, rather than telling them what they should and should not be doing. Youth say they strongly resent having parents and pastors respond to them either in a condescending or judgmental fashion, or by giving ultimatums. Second, teens say they long for guidance from adults. They clearly express this need, despite projecting an exterior image of independence. As one seventeen-year-old male stated at a dating-violence awareness seminar in front of nearly five hundred Christian youth, parents, and pastors, "How are we teens supposed to learn all there is to know about life if you adults won't teach us?" But the young man quickly added, "We need adults to be our loving and respectful guides, not our stern judges." Hundreds of Christian females and males have made similar pleas in my presence during the past five years.

This book offers parents and pastors a number of strategies to help build bridges rather than barriers with the teens in their lives. The primary focus here is on strategies to end violence in teen-dating relationships. This requires that parents and pastors learn more about abusers' emotional, physical, sexual, and spiritual abuse tactics; that they take a close look at how offenders use popular culture and Christian traditions to excuse and justify their violence; and that they allow teens to discuss their own sexuality and share their stories in their own ways.

A word of warning: Teen dating violence is a very dangerous crime. It requires the coordinated efforts of people throughout our community, both laity and professionals, to combat it. Parents and pastors must therefore never attempt to intervene in these situations alone. In addition, teen dating violence can be graphic and repugnant, sometimes involving emotional, physical, and sexual torture. I would perform a disservice to pastors and parents if I attempted to lessen this harsh reality with watered-down stories and deleted words.

What you read in the five chapters of this book will more than likely sicken and may even terrify you. From March 2003 to September 2004, I interviewed more than two hundred young people between the ages of thirteen and twenty-four living in rural, urban, and suburban areas of the United States. Most of these youth and young adults identified themselves as Christians. While I have sometimes changed their names, I have used their exact words. The material is presented in an unedited and matter-of-fact tone. It would be disrespectful to do otherwise because survivors have courageously chosen to educate us with their truths. Besides, an edited version of events would suggest that the audience consists of children, rather than parents and pastors.

Read the book with other parents, clergy, Christian educators, youth, youth ministers, and youth workers. If you become overwhelmed, put the material down from time to time. But please return to it. As parents and pastors, we need to equip ourselves if we are to help the teens we love break free from the clutches of abuse perpetrated by a violent dating partner.

May God bless and strengthen us on every step of our journey.

1.

Hell on Earth:

Violence in the Dating

Relationships of Christian Teens

Qualities of a Healthy Dating Relationship

Seventeen-year-old Rachel DeYoung and nineteen-year-old Jordan Goettsche have never met. They are from different ethnic backgrounds, African-American and white; from different states in the Union; and, while Rachel grew up in a home that espoused Christian values, Jordan was raised in a family where no particular religious tradition was practiced.

What these two young adults share in common is their clear understanding of the qualities necessary to have a healthy teen dating relationship.

"I think there needs to be respect and trust between the two people," says Rachel, a senior at DeLaSalle High School in Minneapolis. "There also needs to be laughter, honesty, and open communication." Jordan, a recent graduate of Kennedy High School in Cedar Rapids, Iowa, agrees. "A healthy teen dating relationship is one where two people enjoy spending time together," he says. "They listen to and talk with each other, and have trust and respect for one another."

Both Jordan and Rachel believe it's important for teens who are dating to maintain relationships with family and friends. "It's very healthy for the couple to still make time for other people," Jordan says. "In this way, they're less likely to become too dependent upon one another." Rachel adds, "There needs to be some sort of limits set. As teenagers, we shouldn't have the person we're dating be the only focus of our lives. We're still pretty young and don't have a lot of experience in life."

Rachel expresses further concern about teens isolating themselves from family and friends during courtship. "We may think this will be the person that we're going to be with forever, but most likely it's not," she says. "If we spend all our time focusing on this one relationship and it ends, then we're somewhat stuck. The friends we used to have, the ones we've pushed away along with our family, are now all hurt by the distance we created. So we now have a lot of repair work to do in order to regain their trust. Isolating ourselves from everyone when we're dating is just not very healthy."

Hell on Earth

Unfortunately, not all teens are experiencing the kind of balance, joy, respect, trust, and warmth just described by Rachel and Jordan. Millions of young women and young men in the United States are secretly living in a type of hell on earth, brought on by the abusive and violent behavior of a dating partner.

Christian youth are not immune to this pervasive problem.

Sarah's Story

"I met Lawrence when I was a seventeen-year-old freshman at the conservative, Christian college we both were attending," recalls Sarah. Now an advocate for teen and adult survivors of intimate partner violence, Sarah was, as a teen, impressed by the charm and persistence of the nineteen-year-old Lawrence.

"He really pursued me, which was very validating," Sarah says. "Lawrence asked people on campus for my phone number. Then he called and left these really nice messages. I knew some of his friends and they'd tell me, 'Lawrence always asks about you. He thinks you're really pretty.' One time Lawrence waited outside my dorm room until I arrived, just to hold open the door for me. He seemed so nervous and shy while trying to strike up a conversation. I thought this behavior was really cute."

The young Christian couple's romance moved along quickly. "After six months of dating, I was definitely in love with Lawrence," Sarah says. "He was so affectionate and always called me 'sweetie' and all these other pet names. Lawrence was involved in ministry and thinking about going into missions work. We had even talked about getting married. Everything seemed so perfect."

Then one day, after Sarah declined Lawrence's invitation to get together at the home of some of their friends, she saw a very different side of her Christian boyfriend. "Lawrence became very upset and called me 'crazy' and 'stupid' and said he could go out with other women who would appreciate him and his life more," Sarah recalls. "I was shocked and hurt by his words. I was really committed to Lawrence and felt we had a deep connection. So immediately I took responsibility for his verbal attack. And I convinced myself that I needed to try harder to make the relationship work."

The abuse Lawrence perpetrated against Sarah quickly escalated. As we'll see throughout the book, Sarah continues to live with the scars caused by the emotional, physical, sexual, and spiritual terror Lawrence inflicted against her.

What Constitutes Teen Dating Violence?

According to the Dating Violence Resource Center, a program of the National Center for Victims of Crime, dating violence is controlling, abusive, and aggressive behavior in a romantic relationship. The problem occurs in both heterosexual and homosexual relationships and can include verbal, emotional, physical, or sexual abuse, or a combination of these.[1]

Any teen can be a victim of dating violence. The problem exists in all cultures, races, socio-economic classes, and religions. Both females and males are victimized. Girls are more likely than are boys to yell, threaten to hurt themselves, pinch, slap, scratch, or kick their partners. Boys injure girls more and are more likely to punch their partners and force them to participate in unwanted sexual activity. Some teen victims experience violence occasionally. Others are abused more often, sometimes daily.[2]

The Dating Violence Resource Center offers these facts about the prevalence of abuse in teen dating relationships:

- 40 percent of teenage girls ages 14 through 17 report knowing someone their age who has been hit or beaten by a boyfriend.[a]
- 50 to 80 percent of teens [boys and girls] report knowing someone involved in a violent relationship.[b]
- Physical aggression occurs in 1 in 3 teen dating relationships.[c]
- 33 percent of teenage girls report experiencing physical violence at the hands of a dating partner.[d]
- Young women ages sixteen through twenty-four experience the highest rates of relationship violence.[e]
- Date rape accounts for almost 70 percent of the sexual assaults reported by adolescent and college-age women.[f]
- Many studies indicate that, as a dating relationship becomes more serious, the potential for and nature of violent behavior also escalates.[g3]

Tactics

Let's look closely at some of the various tactics used by perpetrators of teen dating violence to get what they want from their victims. Stories of victims-survivors and their abusers will be woven together with comments from peer educators and adult professionals in order to provide parents and pastors with a comprehensive overview of the problem. (All the stories are true. In some instances, names of survivors and their perpetrators have been changed to maintain the anonymity of the survivors.)

Verbal Abuse

Verbal abuse is emotionally abusive. However, since emotional abuse is sometimes nonverbal in nature, we'll divide the two types of abuse into separate categories.

> When I was in high school, I witnessed teens in the hall calling each other bad names. Guys would call girls "bitch," "slut," and "tramp." Girls called guys "bastard," "dick head," and "dork." And both girls and guys often said to one another the phrase, "fuck you."
> —Chris Stumpff, 19, Cedar Rapids, Iowa

> At my school, guys call girls "slut," "ho," and "skank." And they refer to some girls as "easy."
> —Vanessa Silver, 17, Norco, California

The invitations I receive from pastors, lay leaders, and teachers at Christian high schools to speak on teen dating violence awareness are often accompanied by one specific request. I'm asked to "tone down" my language during the presentations. Christian youth, these leaders tell me, are not used to the "bad" and "foul" language expressed by many young adults in secular society. Therefore, I need to be careful not to "pollute" the hearts and minds of Christian youth.

I always consent to this request, but with one stipulation: that I'm allowed to ask the young people what negative terms they themselves have heard their Christian peers call one another. Invariably, whether I'm addressing youth in rural, suburban, or urban locales, and while speaking with both Catholic and Protestant teens from a variety of ethnic backgrounds, the words used are the same as those recited by youth in the overall general public. To name just a few: Bastard. Bitch. Crazy. Cunt. Dike. Fag. Fat. Ho. Hoochie. Skank. Slut. Stupid. Tramp. Ugly. Whore.

A Youth Pastor's Story

"I hear the word 'slut' used a lot by some of the teens in my group," says Niki Christiansen. She has served as youth pastor at West Court Street Church of God in Flint, Michigan, for four-and-a-half years. "I also hear the youth using such adjectives as 'cheap' and 'easy' in reference to females they think are sexually promiscuous," she says.

Christiansen says she always tries to address these comments in a pastoral fashion. "Generally, I make some kind of statement to the youth like 'the words or phrases you've just used do not show respect. We can look to Scripture as a basis to demonstrate why we, as Christians, are to watch carefully what we say to others. We need to avoid words or phrases that degrade or hurt another child of God.'"

Christiansen admits that reactions to her approach vary. "Sometimes, the teens will listen to what I have to say and then acknowledge that negative words can be very hurtful to others," she says. "At other times, they look at me and say, 'It's no big deal. They're only words.' It is as though they just want to avoid the discussion altogether."

Actually, verbal abuse is a very big deal. It causes those who receive it to think less of themselves—emotionally, physically, spiritually.

"As our relationship progressed, the names got worse," says Sarah, whom we met earlier in this chapter. She was seventeen when she began dating nineteen-year-old Lawrence, who was both a Christian and an abuser. "I was no longer his 'sweetie,' but instead he started calling me a 'bitch,' a 'cunt,' and told me I was too 'rigid.' The name-calling, along with a lot of nonverbal things he'd do, caused me to doubt and question myself. I felt broken, humiliated, and sad much of the time."

For more than six years, Stephanie Liester has counseled adult and teen women victimized by their male intimate partners. She is the co-clinical director of therapy service for Safe Nest, located in Las Vegas, Nevada. The agency provides temporary assistance for survivors of intimate partner violence. Liester frequently sees teen women who are devastated by being called vile names.

"Verbal abuse has broken the spirits of many of the young women I see," Liester says. "A lot of the teens tell me 'I don't feel good about myself.' 'I don't feel happy.' 'I don't smile anymore.' Often, these young women don't really know why this is the case until we get to the fact that the vile names they've been called by their boyfriends have torn down their confidence, self-esteem, and their overall sense of who they are as individuals."

Liester says the abusive names most frequently used against the girls she sees all have sexual connotations. "The young women are called 'bitch,' 'cunt,' 'slut,' and 'whore.' Personally, I think these terms have the greatest negative impact upon girls and women."

Bitch

The term "bitch" is demeaning and so dehumanizing. It turns females into objects. I can't understand why a whole generation has embraced it. I think it's so bizarre that "bitch" is even being said on TV. I just can't get my mind around it.

—Shari Miller, Community Corrections
Improvement Association, Cedar Rapids, Iowa

The term "bitch" needs further attention because it has seeped into the very fabric of everyday society. "Bitch" now holds a prominent place in the hearts, souls, and vocabulary of many teens, Christians as well as non-Christians.

"The culture has brainwashed kids into thinking that 'bitch' is a good thing; a flattering thing," proclaims Dr. Jill Murray. She's a psychotherapist with a private practice in Laguna Niguel, California. Widely known as the leading expert in the field of teen dating and teen relationship violence awareness, Dr. Murray speaks to more than one hundred thousand teens each year worldwide. She is the author of three volumes dealing with this topic: *But I Love Him: Protecting Your Teen Daughters from Controlling, Abusive, Dating Relationships* (New York: HarperCollins, 2000); *Destructive Relationships: A Guide to Changing the Unhealthy Relationships in Your Life* (San Diego: Jodere, 2002); and *But He's Never Hit Me: The Devastating Costs of Nonphysical Abuse to Girls and Women* (San Diego: Jodere, 2004).

Dr. Murray vividly describes how some teen boys take full advantages of the brainwashing teen girls have received through our society's pervasive use of the term "bitch." "Girls are frequently trained to find 'bitch' both flattering and possessive, as well as a pejorative term," she explains. "It's also a very demeaning way to describe girls and women.

"What I've heard from teenage boys, when they're very honest, is that they find if they can call a girl a 'bitch' and she's okay with it, then these boys know that they can pretty much do whatever they want with these girls. So it's important for both girls and boys to understand that name-calling is really where an abusive relationship starts," Dr. Murray says.

I have a few things I want to say directly to males about use of the term "bitch." When we choose to disrespect any girl or woman by referring to her in such a repugnant manner, in essence we have chosen to defile all females—including our own mothers, wives, daughters, sisters, nieces, friends, neighbors. Ultimately, we do a grave injustice to ourselves as well. We cannot share fully in the blessings that come from being a child of God when we demonstrate such blatant disregard for others of God's creation—females. Boys and men, let's make a powerful and positive statement by forever banishing the word "bitch" from our hearts, souls, and tongues. We can then work toward taking the same stand against all other language designed to put down females.

Emotional Abuse

> A lot of Lawrence's abuse didn't involve name-calling. He'd do many other things to cut me down and humiliate me. For example, he'd take a poem I'd written for him, something deeply personal to which I'd given a lot of effort and in which I expressed my love, and would read it aloud in front of his friends while laughing at me. I felt completely embarrassed and inadequate, both as a writer and as a person.
>
> —Sarah, teen dating abuse survivor

Emotional abuse can include the scathing name-calling just discussed. But in its broader context, emotional abuse can be either devoid of demeaning language or it can be used in conjunction with negative words and a host of other abusive patterns. Let's look closely at some of the additional emotional abuse tactics perpetrators of teen dating violence employ to maintain control of the people they victimize. *Bear in mind that the three major components of an abusive relationship, which Dr. Jill Murray calls the tripod upon which everything else stands, are possessiveness, jealousy, and controlling behaviors.*

Technology – A Modern Day Stalking Tool

The Pager: Amy's Story

At age fourteen, Amy Woods received a pager from her mother. Immediately, her sixteen-year-old boyfriend began using what was then the state-of-the-art technology to take control over her entire being. "He would page me constantly," she says. Even though there were no demands verbalized, Woods says she knew she had a limited time to respond. "If I didn't phone him immediately," she explains, "the pages would become incessant and my boyfriend would become enraged."

Now age twenty-two, Woods works tirelessly to help free other young women from the claws of possessive and controlling boyfriends. She's an advocate for teens and a case manager with the Domestic Violence Clearinghouse and Legal Hotline in Honolulu. Still, she often reflects upon the abusive relationship in her past, and on how a pager—something her mother gave her to keep connected to loved ones in positive ways—became a weapon used against her.

"I'd be at school in a class and my pager would go off," Woods recalls. "Immediately, I would try to leave the room to respond. But, if I couldn't, the pager would go off again in about five minutes. And, if I didn't phone him back, the pager would go off again in another minute. Then the pages would come twice a minute, then three times a minute, then for as many times as he could page me within a minute."

Woods says the pager displayed not only a dial back number, but also abusive coded messages. "My boyfriend and I used numbers as codes," Woods explains. "He'd spell out a sentence with those numbers. Certain numbers can look like certain letters when they're upside-down or backward. So my boyfriend would literally spell out 'Fuck you,' 'You bitch,' 'Wait 'til you come home,' 'You're an asshole.'"

Asked to reflect as a twenty-two-year-old woman upon her feelings and thoughts about the abuse tactics her boyfriend used against her when she was fourteen, Woods said, "At the time, I do remember having an uncomfortable feeling, but my response to that uncomfortable feeling was always, 'I have to call him back.' That was it. I didn't see outside the box. I didn't see beyond the scene of him paging me. Certainly, I was uncomfortable with what he was doing, but my focus was on doing what he wanted me to do."

Cell Phones, an Even More Sophisticated Weapon

> I'm seeing a young lady right now whose parents got her last two cell phone bills. There were more than sixteen hundred incoming text messages in one month, and more than one hundred phone calls.
>
> —Dr. Jill Murray, Psychotherapist

Pagers are used far less frequently than they were when Amy Woods was a teen. Nowadays, cell phones have become the preferred way to achieve, as the popular ad says, "global communication." Cell phones have also replaced pagers as the number-one weapon used by perpetrators of teen dating violence to insure possession of and total control over their intimate partners.

Dr. Jill Murray describes a common misuse of cell phone technology, in this case by teen boys, to guarantee total power over their female intimate partners. "I'm now finding something particularly heinous: A boy will call a girl on her cell phone at all hours of the night. This is such a familiar story that it's now become the norm in an abusive relationship. Usually a teenage girl, even if she has a phone in her room, can't receive calls in the middle of the night. The parents would hear the phone ringing. So her boyfriend tells her to sleep on her back with the cell phone on her chest set to vibrate."

Dr. Murray explains the vast negative impact this type of situation has upon the body, mind, and spirit of the girl. "His behavior completely overpowers and controls her, making her feel worthless," Murray says. "She's been totally objectified by him. He completely dismisses her right to privacy and her need for sleep. It doesn't matter if she has a test the next morning, or if he's already kept her on the phone until midnight to harass her, or make her answer for actions or things she didn't do. All that matters is that she has to be available to him around the clock. And, if he can't be with her every moment of every day, the cell phone guarantees she can never escape his possessive and controlling behavior, which is really criminal in nature."

Jealousy, Possessiveness, Controlling Behaviors— No Connection to Love

At one point during their courtship, seventeen-year-old Sarah caught her nineteen-year-old boyfriend, Lawrence, flirting with another young woman. She decided to confront his behavior. "He just went hysterical," Sarah recalls. "Lawrence started throwing things, and crying, and ranting and raving. I was trying to calm him down; his mother was trying to calm him down. And, even though I was right there with him, he was calling me on my phone and leaving messages, 'I love you . . . this is why I'm so upset.'"

When he finally calmed down, Lawrence began providing Sarah with a laundry list of unfaithfulness. "He said that his whole life had been ruined by cheating. His dad had cheated on his mom, his former girlfriend had cheated on him, and so, he said, he was reacting out of those past hurts. He didn't want our relationship to end up like that."

Even though Sarah says she found Lawrence's reactions to her confrontation both abnormal and very odd, she admits to taking full responsibility for his behavior. "I told him I didn't think my question would upset him so much, and that I didn't realize he loved me so much and was that committed to me. I then apologized for ever questioning him."

Popular culture and Christian teachings often work against teens' ability to gain a healthy understanding of themselves as unique and valued members of society. In the story just told, Sarah's questioning of Lawrence over what she observed as his flirtatious behavior with another woman somehow ended with Sarah apologizing. On the other hand, Sarah interprets Lawrence's histrionics as a demonstration of love and commitment rather than as manipulative and controlling behavior that helped him to escape accountability for his actions.

In today's society, jealousy, possessiveness, and controlling behaviors are too often equated with love. An intimate partner who dictates choice of clothing, friends, food, hairstyle, and the amount of time spent with family is, at least initially, thought by some teens to be cute, romantic, sexy, and a positive sign from God. Take note of the responses I received at a Christian high school when I asked teens the following question: What would be your reaction to having a jealous, possessive, or controlling boyfriend or girlfriend?

- It would show how much a girl loves me if she wanted to know where I was at all times, and who I was with.
- If a guy is jealous, that tells me that he's really sensitive and not afraid to show how much he cares.
- If a guy wants to possess me, I'd think that's so romantic.
- If a girl is jealous, I wouldn't have to worry about her cheating on me.
- I like "take control" types of guys. I know then that they'll protect me from anything.
- I want a guy who I can serve. He is my head, and I want to respect his position of authority, just like the Bible teaches.

In the next chapter, we'll explore further the major role popular culture and Christian teachings have in shaping what teens feel and think about healthy and unhealthy dating relationships.

Threats—Always to be Taken Seriously

> He never threatened to kill me or my family or friends. Instead he'd say, "I'd never hurt you. But, if you ever break up with me, I'm going to kill myself and it'll be your fault."
>
> —Angie, teen dating violence survivor

Threats to harm oneself or others are common emotional abuse tactics. They are used both by female and male teens. Girls are more likely than boys to threaten to hurt themselves. Threats must always be taken seriously. Angie, a nineteen-year-old teen dating violence survivor, knows this from firsthand experience.

Angie's Story

"Our relationship was like something out of a love story," Angie recalls, referring to the beginnings of her courtship with a young man named Paul. She was thirteen at the time, and he was fifteen. "Paul was so good to me. He'd draw me pictures, write poems, and do a lot of other nice things. For instance, he wanted to pick me up and take me to school every day."

Within weeks, Paul was telling Angie he was in love with her. "I was shocked and confused," Angie says. "At age thirteen, I didn't have a clue what being in love meant. Paul told me this over the telephone, and I remember replying, 'Uh, me too!' I didn't say, 'I love you, too' because like I just said, I didn't even know what love was about. Yet, at the same time, it was good to hear those words from Paul. I felt real special."

Paul's quick declaration of love soon was accompanied by his dictation of Angie's clothing and friendships. "I'd visit my friends, and Paul would just drop by and take me away," Angie recalls. "He didn't like my friends or any of the other people I'd talk to. He also didn't like the clothing or make-up I wore. When I dressed in shorts, he was especially upset saying, 'You dress just like a ho.' This behavior caused me to begin to wonder if Paul really loved and respected me, like he always claimed. Or, did he do all these things because he was a jerk?"

Paul's physical abuse of Angie began shortly thereafter. "I'd do something that bothered him, though I could never tell what set him off," Angie says. "And Paul would always grab my wrist real hard, push me against a wall, and say 'Why do you do all these things to upset me?' He'd be yelling so loudly right in my face, and it was very hard to calm him down."

Paul's emotional and physical abuse continued and, after nearly two years, Angie sought to end the relationship. "It felt like I was being brainwashed," Angie says. "One minute Paul would literally lock me in a room because he didn't like the clothing I was going to wear to school, and the next he'd say, 'Oh, I'm so sorry, Baby. I'm just trying to look out for you because I know how guys are with girls. They don't have good intentions.'"

Angie says Paul offered her a chilling warning when he sensed she was drawing away from him. "He said, 'I'd never hurt you. But, if you break up with me, I'm going to kill myself, and it's going to be your fault.'" Despite this threat, Angie ended her two-year dating relationship with Paul. A week later, he showed up at her home, unannounced. He begged his former girlfriend to take him back. "He was saying, 'I'm nothing without you. Do you think some other guy is going to love you the way I do? Please take me back. I promise to change.'"

Angie remained strong in her conviction to end the relationship. "I had a real weak spot in my heart for Paul because I did really care for him," she says. "But I knew I had to get out of that relationship; it was not healthy. So I told Paul he needed to leave my home immediately. But he refused. Instead, he fell to his knees and cried and pleaded all the more."

Several people arrived at Angie's home to try and persuade her ex-boyfriend to vacate the premises. Hours later, Paul promised Angie he'd leave on his own if she spent a few moments alone with him. "I believed Paul's promise," Angie says. "I told everyone things would be fine. So, except for one of Paul's male cousins, who went to the back room to watch TV, everybody left the house."

Paul suggested to Angie that they talk in the garage, where there was a bed to sit on. "He asked me one more time to take him back. When I refused, he stood up and pulled something bright and shiny out of his pocket. Quickly, I realized it was a butcher knife from my kitchen."

Angie sustained fifteen stab wounds from Paul; at least two of these were potentially fatal, according to doctors treating her. Miraculously, she suffers no physical limitations from Paul's brutal attack. But, emotionally, she struggles. "I keep wondering why my ex-boyfriend, the man who said he loved me so much and promised never to hurt me, tried to take my life." And, as we'll see in chapter 5, Angie's spiritual scars also run very deep.

Physical Abuse

Fifty sixteen-year-old young men and women at a Christian high school gave these responses to the question of when it is acceptable to use physical force against a boyfriend or girlfriend:

- When she disappoints him
- When he cheats on her
- When she flirts with another guy
- When he's being a jerk
- When she disobeys him
- When he calls her bad names
- When she calls him a "fag" or a "queer"
- When he hits her first
- When she hits him first
- When he doesn't pay enough attention to her
- Never

These replies are not uncommon. In fact, adolescent girls and boys make similar statements during most of the teen dating violence awareness sessions I conduct in parochial and public schools, and with church youth groups. Therefore, conversations about physical abuse tactics perpetrated both by females and males are essential.

Violence is always an inappropriate way to deal with conflict. This truth is the same for young children, adolescents, and adults. Often, a teenage boy or girl will attempt to justify an act of physical aggression by saying "I was angry." It is important that we point out to these young women and men that anger is a feeling while violence is a behavior. All of us have a right to what we feel. It is unacceptable to respond to these feelings in an abusive manner. As adults, we must help teens find alternatives to the violence many of them are perpetrating.

Sexual Abuse and Assault

With regards to teen pregnancy related to teen sexual assault, I have contact with a victim who is a Protestant Christian. This young woman was terrified to tell her parents—not so much about the attack, but about the pregnancy. She said she feared that, no matter the circumstances, the parents and entire church would be upset with her for having sex.

—Amy Woods, teen dating violence survivor and advocate with the Domestic Violence Clearinghouse and Legal Hotline, Honolulu

Many of the parents and pastors who attend the sessions I facilitate on teen dating violence awareness freely admit to feeling uncomfortable discussing the topics of sexual abuse and sexual assault. As one Christian mother of a fifteen-year-old girl disclosed recently, "Somehow, I keep telling myself that if my daughter doesn't have sex until she's married, then there's no need to worry about some boy sexually abusing or assaulting her." This statement reveals some all-too-common misconceptions about what actually constitutes sexual abuse and sexual assault within a teen dating relationship. There is widespread belief that these problems are related to consensual sexual activities, or solely to sexual intercourse, or to the timeworn myth that they are caused by what the young woman was doing, saying, or wearing. In addition, there is the common myth that sexual abuse and sexual assault are related to the broader concept of human sexuality, which we will discuss throughout the remaining chapters of the book. None of these assumptions is accurate.

Facts
Sexual abuse and sexual assault in teen dating relationships are crimes perpetrated primarily by males against females. As mentioned at the beginning of this chapter, date rape accounts for almost 70 percent of the sexual assaults reported by adolescent and college-age women.

Definitions of Sexual Abuse and Sexual Assault

Erica Staab Westmoreland works as the Sexual Assault Coordinator for the South Carolina Coalition Against Domestic Violence and Sexual Assault. "When we are speaking of sexual assault, we're referring to something that has happened once," she says, after being asked to define the term. "When we are speaking of sexual abuse, we're referring to something that has happened repeatedly."

Sexual abuse and sexual assault occur on a continuum. "These behaviors often begin with forcing someone to look at or listen to something they don't want to," Westmoreland explains. She used as an example a teen girl being forced by her teen boyfriend to look at a pornographic magazine or video, or being asked by the boy to participate in some type of phone sex activity that she finds objectionable.

Many people think only of unwanted sexual intercourse when asked to define sexual abuse tactics. Westmoreland reveals that a wide range of additional behaviors fit into this category. "These tactics include touching, pinching, or grabbing another person in private areas like their breast, buttocks, or genitals," she says, "or forcing someone to perform sexual acts. As stated earlier, when sexual activity is forced, either physically or with fear or intimidation, and it occurs one time, that's sexual assault. If the forced sexual activity occurs repeatedly, it's sexual abuse."

Sexual Activity among Teens: Consensual or Coercive?

Laws vary from state to state regarding when a sexual relationship can be considered consensual. Westmoreland points out, for example, that in her state of residence, South Carolina, the age of consent is sixteen, while in New York it is age seventeen. Legally, adolescents cannot be in a consensual sexual relationship, not even if they say they're a willing participant, if they are under the state designated age of consent. Therefore, parents and pastors need to verify the laws in their particular state.

In addition to the varying laws covering age of consent, Westmoreland addresses other factors to consider when determining if sexual activity between teens is consensual. "Both parties need to be free to change their mind at any point," she says. "And, at any time, they each need to be able to say no. Their partner must immediately accept and respect this no, without attempting to coerce or manipulate the other's decision. And they both need to be fully awake."

Teen boys use various tactics to coerce teen girls into sexual activity. "There is a very strong push in teen culture, and especially on the part of abusive boys, not to listen to or respect a girl's request not to be sexual," says Dr. Jill Murray. "So an abusive boy will most commonly request sexual intercourse. And, if a girl says no because she doesn't feel ready or that she has decided to wait until after marriage, then the abusive boy may choose to say something crass—and it is a choice because all abuse is intentional. He'll say something like, 'Okay, if you're not ready to have sexual intercourse, then just give me a blow job or a hand job.' And the girl doesn't realize that he is actually raping her; it's coercive sex because he has chosen not to respect her desire not to be sexual."

Erica Staab Westmoreland adds: "I see girls, especially younger age teens, who are dating older males," she says. "These girls are being told 'You can't get pregnant because it's your first time.' Or 'If we stand up while we're having sex you won't get pregnant.' Or 'Anal sex and oral sex aren't really like having sex. We can do these things, and you'll still maintain your virginity.' These older teen men prey upon the inexperience of younger teen women to coerce them into engaging in sexual activities."

Westmoreland, who is herself a Christian, discusses one sexual abuse tactic boys use—especially on teen girls who are Christians. "If a boy and girl have done things that are considered against the rules of church, home, or school," she explains, "then the boy will often threaten to expose the girl—unless she agrees to his sexual demands. 'If you don't have intercourse or oral sex with me,' he'll say, 'then I'm going to tell your parents, pastors, and friends what we've already done.' Or 'I'm going to tell everyone we've already been having sex—so you might as well agree to do it.'" Westmoreland says she hears these types of stories on a regular basis.

When Consensual Sex Turns Abusive

Some Christian male teens use sexual abuse tactics against their female teen intimate partners. Here's what happened in one such situation:

Sarah's Story II

> Lawrence and I decided to engage in sexual intercourse six months into our dating relationship. The choice was mutual. Having been raised in strict, conservative Christian homes, this decision caused both of us to feel somewhat guilty. For me, I realized I was breaking one of the three big rules taught by my Christian denomination—the other two being alcohol or drug use. I think Lawrence dealt with his guilt by keeping our having sex a big secret. He didn't even tell his closest male friends. In fact, when I told our mutual friends we were having sex, he would deny it to them. And he used to say to me that if his mother found out she would die. Literally die, he said; and I believed him.
>
> Lawrence was a big guy who lifted weights. By this time in the relationship, he began on occasion to hold me against the wall and scream obscenities in my face when he was angry with me. He'd tell me how mad he was over something I'd done. Or that I wasn't being kind enough to his family. I was absolutely terrified by his physical show of force. He would use every ounce of his strength to keep

me pinned against the wall. It was very frightening. During sex, Lawrence would at first be very affectionate and tender. But then, all of a sudden, he'd switch and want us to engage in what he called a "game." As a type of foreplay, Lawrence would hold me down on the bed—with as much force as he used to pin me against the wall when he was angry—and make me try to escape. Or he'd put a finger on my chest and would demand that I attempt to get away from him. The harder I tried to escape, the more Lawrence would hold me down with his big, muscular body. All the while, he'd become more and more angry.

On several occasions, Lawrence had threatened to kill himself. He sometimes even incorporated this threat into the so-called "game" he had set up during sex by keeping a gun by the bed. Or he'd cover my face with his hands or pillows and would call me "lazy cunt" and yell "Don't look at me. Stop looking at me!" One time I told Lawrence that his behavior was scaring me. And he said it was the way he had always made love. He also said that he felt guilty, as a Christian, about having sex before marriage, and said something to the effect that he was either going to stop his abusive behavior during sex or stop having sex altogether until we got married. But he'd then quickly add, "I know sex is what you want." So he minimized his abusive behavior, my feelings, and he blamed me for the mutual decision we had made to have sexual intercourse.

Warning Signs

In Cedar Rapids, Iowa, a group of young adults formed Ta Da (Teens Against Domestic Abuse and Violence). They speak regularly to other teens, at schools and church youth gatherings, as well as with adults about teen dating violence awareness. Chris Stumpff, age nineteen, is one of the members of Ta Da. He describes a skit he and his colleagues wrote, which opens every presentation.

A guy and a girl meet each other at a bowling alley. He gets her phone number and, after a few weeks, they start dating. The next scene, they are eating at a restaurant. The guy orders a salad for the girl—with light dressing. He tells her she needs to go on a diet because she's putting on too much weight.

The next night, the girl is out at a pizza parlor with her girlfriends. The guy calls her cell phone and hears a waiter talking in the background and assumes that his girlfriend is out with some other guy. He feels jealous and begins yelling at her before he hangs up the phone.

Later that night, when the girl arrives home, her boyfriend is there waiting for her. She tries to hug him, but he pushes her away, calls her a tramp, and then tells her that he's going to find the guy she was with and kill him. Then, he says, he's going to kill her, too.

The next night, the young woman is in her bedroom working on a school project with a girlfriend. The friend notices that she has a large bruise on one of her hands. She asks how it got there.

We then divide the audience into small groups and ask them to discuss how they themselves would respond to the abused teen. Some attendees then volunteer to participate in a process Ta Da uses, which is a form of Interactive Theater. This is a way for people to explore difficult subjects in a safe way. It is experiential learning, which, for many kids, is more effective than just talking.

More than thirty-five teens, Christians and non-Christians, attended a workshop I had the privilege of co-facilitating with Ta Da. When the audience divided into small groups following the bowling alley skit, I asked attendees to identify the first warning sign that indicated to them that the young woman might be abused by her boyfriend. Most of the teens said their first indicator was the bruise on the young woman's hand; some said it was when her boyfriend called her a "tramp"; a few identified the boyfriend's phone call to the pizza parlor as the initial warning; and fewer still said they thought the first indication of abuse was when the boy dictated what the young woman could eat and when he made negative comments about her weight.

The above responses serve as a microcosm to the multiplicity of subtle and overt warning signs parents and pastors must be on the lookout for that may indicate teen girls or boys are being violated by a dating partner. Claire Woods knows all about these indicators and how a victimized teen can participate in trying to hide the abuse. She is the mother of Amy, the teen dating abuse survivor whom we first met earlier in the chapter.

Claire Woods's Story
"We really liked the young man Amy was dating. He had come from a real troubled home. And, I think being caring parents and Christians, we thought that maybe we could do something for him. Our home was a place of refuge. His parents argued all the time and, when his father was drinking, he often got hit. He was a very sweet and enchanting boy who, in many ways, looked vulnerable. He always showed a great deal of respect to my husband and me."

However, Claire says she began to notice a lot of arguments between this young man and Amy. "They showed no regard for anything," she says. "Even on public streets or over the telephone or in our home, they would openly yell at one another."

Claire admits that often times she and her husband sided more with the young man than with their own daughter. "We defended him more than Amy because she can be pretty overbearing and strong," she says. "When I saw him, he was a good kid and, as I said earlier, he treated my husband and me with the utmost respect. This was not someone who you wouldn't want your daughter with—he seemed like such a nice kid."

Over time, Claire says, she began to observe a different side of this young man. "A lot of control and intimidation," is how she now describes his behavior. "And I would hear him say to my daughter 'You're stupid! Why don't you just do what I tell you?' Amy is very bright, beautiful, and talented, and she excelled in school. She deserved far better treatment than what she was receiving from her boyfriend—and I began to tell her this." Amy did not respond well to her mother's words. "She would either defend him or find a reason that his abusive behavior was her fault," Claire says. "And usually she'd then walk away from me."

Unexplained bruises began to appear on Amy's body. Claire confronted her daughter once again. But the teen always had an explanation. "In hindsight, I see that the abuse was very hard to detect. Amy was a master of hiding a lot of the abuse," Claire says. "And, if she didn't hide it, she had valid explanations as to how the bruises got on her body. For example, there was once a bruise on her cheek, and she told us that the car door opened suddenly and hit her in the face. Well, our car door actually does open suddenly like that. So I thought her explanation was pretty legitimate. But I don't think my husband bought into Amy's explanations for a minute. He was on to what was actually happening to our daughter a whole lot sooner than I was. If anybody was in denial, it was me."

Here are some common warning signs that may indicate a teen girl or teen boy is in an abusive dating relationship:

- Radical change in behavior—teen seems anxious, depressed, hypersensitive, withdrawn
- Ceases activities once enjoyed
- Distances self from family and friends—especially if teen previously enjoyed a close relationship with these individuals

- Decrease in academic performance
- Seems uninterested in physical appearance or personal hygiene
- Dresses inappropriately for the season or situation—wears coats, heavy jackets, sweaters, or sweatshirts in summer weather; or wears sunglasses on cloudy or rainy days or indoors
- Receives an inordinate number of phone calls from dating partner—or partner always seems to be around
- Seems afraid of dating partner, or either defends or takes the blame for partner's bad behavior
- Secretiveness
- Has unexplained bruises, or offers unbelievable or vague explanations for bruises

It is important to understand not all the above red flags point to abuse. "Some warning signs are hard to differentiate for parents and pastors as to what's normal in teenage years and what's the result of abuse," says Dr. Jill Murray. "As kids age, they do become more secretive, for example, and do separate from their family. So most kids spend less time with their parents at age sixteen, than they did, say, when they were ten. But abuse happens in conjunction with other things. So let's say a girl becomes more secretive; she makes excuses for her boyfriend's poor behavior or blames herself for his poor behavior; she starts diminishing herself as a person; and she's receiving forty phone calls from him every day. Together, these warning signs add up to the likelihood that she's dating an abusive partner."

Conclusion

Hell on Earth. It's a fitting description of the real-life nightmare faced by teens involved with an abusive dating partner. What ought to be one of the most carefree periods of life—adolescence—is made an inferno of verbal, emotional, physical, and sexual torture by an abusive partner. Many survivors say it will take years for them to piece back together their shattered body, mind, and spirit. Some believe they will never be the same.

It would take a great deal of denial and naïveté to think that Christian young adults are somehow immune to the problems associated with teen dating violence. Why would they be? In reality, there are young women and young men attending our congregations, youth groups, and parochial schools who are being abused by, or are the abusers of, a teen dating partner. Hell on Earth, indeed. But the hopeful news is we can help teens out of the darkness. However, if we are to assist in ending violence in teen dating relationships, we must first accept the solemn truth that situations of dating violence exist among us.

Questions for Discussion

1. What are the tactics a perpetrator of teen dating violence uses to control and dominate their dating partner? Describe in detail at least two components that help define each tactic.

2. Are teens in your own congregation facing the problem of dating violence? If yes, what are you and other church members doing to address this matter? If not, how has this pervasive issue evaded you?

3. What did you feel and think as you read Sarah's story? How would you support Sarah, spiritually and emotionally?

4. Which four warning signs indicating the possibility of teen dating violence trouble you most? Tell why.

5. As a result of reading this chapter, what will you do differently as a parent or pastor to address the issue of teen dating violence? Be specific.

2.

How Christian Teachings and Popular Culture Contribute to Teen Dating Violence

As a boy, I was taught by society that men should be dominant in male/female relationships. Men run the family, I was told. Women, on the other hand, should stay home, take care of the kids, and look after and obey their men. If a woman had to take a job outside the home, she should make less money than a man.
—Jordan Goettsche, 19, Cedar Rapids, Iowa

In the Christian tradition in which I was raised, females didn't have a lot of rights—at home or in the church. We weren't able to participate in or make certain decisions in the home, like how and where money was spent. There were very few freedoms I had as a female.
—Sarah, teen dating violence survivor

In this chapter we'll discuss some of the messages from both the Christian church and popular culture that contribute to abuse and violence in teen dating relationships. Although many of these teachings overlap, let us first consider the negative messages expressed by Christian clergy and laity. As in chapter 1, some of the individuals whose stories are told here have been given assumed names in order to protect their anonymity.

Modern-Day Christian Messages

As was vividly illustrated through Sarah's and Amy's stories in chapter 1, Christian youth are very vulnerable to the problem of teen dating violence. Their struggles are often exacerbated by the fact that many Christian adults—parents, pastors, and lay people—deny that the problem exists among churchgoing young people. Some Christians label dating violence a "secular problem." This willful blindness can be likened to a person shouting from a sailboat as a hurricane approaches, "If I just close my eyes, perhaps the storm will simply blow over me!" The raging tropical winds of verbal, emotional, physical, and sexual violence that Christian teens face will not be calmed by this naïve proclamation. If we are to provide safety and shelter to young people caught in the widespread storm of abuse, Christians must first be prepared.

Let us then open our eyes, hearts, and spirits to some of the negative messages teens are receiving from Christian teachings.

Sexuality—"Wait 'til Adulthood or After Marriage"

> My experience, having been raised in the Catholic Christian faith, is that the female body is holy and should be saved for the special union of marriage. Men and boys, on the other hand, still get the message from popular society that they can express themselves sexually. So girls and women still have the undue responsibility to be the gatekeepers of their bodies and uphold a double standard, while the "boys will be boys" rule prevails.
>
> —Grace Alvaro Caligtan, program coordinator of the Teen Alert Program of the Domestic Violence Clearinghouse and Legal Hotline, Honolulu

Many adult Christians want to avoid the topic of teen sexuality altogether. We are either totally uncomfortable with the subject or believe that discussing it with young people will lead them to engage in sexual activities, maybe even intercourse. Thus, many Christian parents defer the discussion until their offspring reach adulthood or after they are married.

"The whole idea of sexuality in teen dating relationships is uncomfortable for most Christians because it requires a very personal discussion," says Pastor Rick Roberts of Kenosha, Wisconsin. For the past eight years he has served as a children's minister. Currently, Roberts is pastor of children and family ministries at Kenosha Bible Church.

Pastor Rick, as parishioners call him, describes what generally happens when Christian leaders and parents decide not to take a proactive role in helping young adults learn about human sexuality. "The kids are left with negative influences from the media and from their peers," he says. "Certainly, Scripture does not shy away from discussing sexuality. But it is an uncomfortable topic for many church leaders and laity, so our kids are not properly nurtured in this area."

Melissa Thielhelm and her husband, Brian, co-direct children and youth ministries at Hope Reformed Church in Sheboygan, Wisconsin. She also sees great risks in Christian teens acquiring their knowledge about sexuality from popular culture. "It seems as though every television channel has a girl or young woman in a two-piece swimsuit, getting either a makeover or implants somewhere," she says. "My husband and I just spoke with members of our youth group. They told us that the kids who are popular 'do sexual stuff.' The youth didn't further explain what that meant. Some of the girls in the group admitted that they wanted to be popular while, at the same time, not wanting to sexually 'cross the line.' As Christian leaders and laity, I don't think we want the popular culture to define for our youth when and where that sexual line is crossed."

Erica Staab Westmoreland from the South Carolina Coalition Against Domestic Violence and Sexual Assault, cautions Christian parents and pastors to remain open to discussing sexuality with young people. "As Christians, we must remember that if we judge kids just because they're sexual beings, then they might not come to us with struggles concerning their sexuality," she says. "There have been so many times I've asked young Christian women if they've spoken with their parents or faith leaders about sexual matters, and they've replied, 'I tried to, but all they did was recite Scripture and tell me what I should and shouldn't be doing.' In every instance, the young women said, these types of responses shut them down."

It is unrealistic to think that Christian youth aren't struggling with the same issues all other young adults face regarding human sexuality. We are sexual beings—just as we're emotional, physical, and spiritual beings. Parents and pastors need to take the lead in discussions on teen sexuality. When we refuse to do so, our teens will turn to their peers or various segments of popular culture to seek direction on this matter. If we want to help Christian teens gain a healthier view on the joys and responsibilities associated with their sexuality, parents and spiritual leaders must talk openly with them about this important aspect of life.

Here is one example why adult Christians need to be actively involved in the nurturing of Christian teens regarding the topic of human sexuality. When youth turn to peers and popular culture for guidance on this matter, they get distorted views on appropriate boundaries. Read the responses of fifty sixteen-year-olds at a Christian high school when they were asked to give examples of situations where they believe a young man or young woman could continue a "sexual activity" even though their partner asked them to stop:

- When she's being a "tease"
- When he's horny
- When she's cheated on him
- When she makes him angry
- When he needs sex
- When he's given her a dozen red roses
- When he's taken her out to a really nice restaurant
- When he buys her an expensive gift
- When she's wearing something really "hot"
- Never

Note that both genders identified situations in which teen males could go beyond the boundaries set by teen females. And, not surprisingly, teens blamed females for their own victimization.

Females Should Save or Rescue Males

Kim Taylor is a Christian and the program director with the Corona, California, office of Alternatives to Domestic Violence. She has direct oversight for the agency's many programs—one of which focuses on teen dating violence prevention. Taylor and her staff see a lot of teens who were raised in church homes. She talks about Christian young women taking on the role of savior or rescuer with abusive Christian and non-Christian male partners.

"We call this 'missionary dating,'" Taylor explains. "For instance, a Christian girl is in a dating relationship with a guy whom she begins to recognize is not really following the Christian path he claims to be taking. The girl then takes on the frame of mind 'Well, I'll pray for him because he doesn't have anybody else.' Or 'I'm going to have to help out because he says I'm the only one who cares about and understands him.' The girl actually begins to take on responsibility for the abusive boy's salvation and well being."

Taylor says some abused Christian teen girls in her program also take Scripture out of its proper context. "A teen girl might tell us, 'Since there's no one else who cares for my boyfriend, then I need to forgive the mean way he's been treating me because Jesus instructs us to forgive seventy times seven.' The girl misapplies the sacred texts to the dysfunction in her intimate relationship. We see this a lot—girls in a savior mode, trying to rescue the very person who is abusing her, instead of separating herself from him."

Amy Woods, the teen dating violence survivor whom we first met in chapter 1, admits to taking on the role of rescuer with her abusive boyfriend. When she was fourteen, he was sent to a youth correctional facility for possession of marijuana. While he was incarcerated, Amy wrote him a letter declaring her desire to have an intimate relationship with him when he was released. "The very day he got the letter he called and said he loved me," Woods recalls. "He also told me I had been the only one to stand by him the three-and-a-half months he'd been away. 'I'm only going to be with you now,' he said. 'You've been the only one who cares about and supports me. I love you.' That gave me another role: to be his savior."

When asked to elaborate, Amy said, "It wasn't that I saw my boyfriend as a non-Christian. He was someone whom I loved that was really hurting. And I very much wanted to help him. I'd grown up in a Catholic Christian family. My parents always taught me to love and help everybody. So I translated all that into trying to help my boyfriend. I convinced myself if I could teach him all my parents had taught me, then I could save him."

There are many pitfalls associated with the savior/ rescuer model described by Kim Taylor and Amy Woods. First, it sets up female Christian teens for failure. True salvation or health *(shalom)*, according to Christian tradition, requires several steps: accepting full responsibility for wrongdoing, being remorseful, facing justice (which may include jail time, paying for the counseling of the person violated, and other financial restitutions) and repentance, which is making a 180-degree turn away from our sins or wrongdoing. None of these steps is the responsibility of—or can be carried out by—anyone but the perpetrator.

The second problem with the savior/rescuer model is that it doesn't hold the abusive male teen accountable for his actions. If he isn't "saved" or "rescued" by the love and support of his female Christian girlfriend (which he won't be!) then she will be blamed. If he's feeling depressed, jealous, insecure, or chooses again to be abusive toward her (remember, the use of violence is always a choice), then she will be blamed.

For Amy Woods, the rescuer role she took on with her ex-boyfriend worked fabulously—at first. "My mother was kind of resistant to my dating him because she knew the trouble he'd gotten into with drugs," Amy says. "But again, being a good Christian woman, she would always give people more and more chances. She would never lose hope in people." The young man even started participating in Woods family activities. "Family is a big part of my life," Amy says, "and my boyfriend willingly interacted with my mom and dad. He even attended church with us."

But after several months, Amy's boyfriend began to abuse her. "He started to tell me to shut up or used other tactics to silence me," Amy says. "I can now see this is disrespectful because he was quieting my beliefs. And, instead of expressing his love in affectionate ways, suddenly he started telling me I was a bitch, an asshole, and stupid."

Gradually, Amy's boyfriend added physical violence to the emotional and verbal abuse he inflicted on her. He once kicked Amy in the chest, and would often slap her with his open hand across the face. Sometimes, he'd take off his beach slippers and use them as a weapon. "The slippers took up more space than his hands," Amy says, "so they caused an even more powerful impact to my face."

After a severe physical beating, Amy eventually broke free of her violent boyfriend. She now helps other violated teen and adult women achieve their freedom. Still, as she reflects on her adolescent years, she clearly understands that she tried to be her boyfriend's rescuer.

> When my boyfriend's apologies would come, it reminded me why I loved him. He did not abuse me twenty-four hours a day. There were days during the week that he was the guy that I was deeply in love with—even though he was abusive and violent and was so scary. But he would apologize, and would even cry, and, with the gifts, and the nice things he'd say and do afterward, he was the sweetest, kindest, and gentlest person. He'd tell me I was the only person who loved and understood him. All this would wipe the slate clean.

Males Are Dominant, Females Are Subordinate—A Spiritually Scarring Experience

Ruth's and Tony's Story
When couples ask me to officiate at their wedding ceremonies, I ask them to take part in three ninety-minute premarital counseling sessions. During these meetings we address such topics as commitment, covenant, equality, love, mutuality, respect, responsibility, and trust. We also talk about domestic violence. There is no place for this criminal and sinful behavior, I tell each couple; marriage is a sacred bond they are making with each other before God.

An eighteen-year-old woman and man, let's call them Ruth and Tony, asked me to officiate at their wedding ceremony. Having been a longtime colleague of Ruth's parents, I gladly agreed. Tony and Ruth came to my office shortly thereafter for the first of their three premarital sessions. The meeting was very congenial, at least until I asked the couple what each of them was vowing to one another. Tony spoke first.

"I promise to be faithful and loving to Ruth, and to always bring home my entire paycheck to provide for the financial needs of my family," Tony proudly replied. He then chose to also speak for his soon-to-be bride. "And Ruth promises to honor and obey me, and to submit to my God-given authority in all things." Tenderly holding hands, the couple then offered each other a glance with the kind of warmth I'd pray for all intimate partners. But despite their obvious affection, I was very uncomfortable with the male hierarchical structure Tony prescribed. Faithfulness, financial security, and love are certainly important aspects of any marriage, I silently mused; still, I needed to hear more from the young Christian man about his day-to-day responsibility to his fiancée.

"Tony, please say more about what you're vowing to Ruth," I requested. "For instance, you mentioned your bride is going to honor, obey, and submit to your God-given authority. Are you planning to do the same for her?" My question seemed to shock Tony. His fair skin rapidly became redder. He looked immediately to Ruth—not with the warm bliss of a moment earlier, but with the kind of frown that said "Honey, please help me explain our position." Ruth looked at me quizzically. My eyes remained fixed on Tony. After what seemed like five minutes of squirming in his chair, the young man finally responded to my query.

"Uh, uh, Reverend Al," Tony began nervously, "Ruth and I both believe in the biblical mandate found in the book of Ephesians, chapter 5, verses 21 through 33. The passage states clearly that Christian wives have to submit graciously to their husbands' authority in all things." I explained to Tony that the text he cited actually provides guidance and instructions not only to Christian wives, but also to Christian husbands. Mutual love, mutual respect, and mutual responsibility are key virtues in a Christian marriage, I said; God views females and males as having equal power and equal value. In addition, I reminded Tony that nine of the twelve verses in Ephesians

5:21-33 are instructions for husbands to follow. Christian men, I asserted, are to love their wives like they love their own bodies, just as Christ loves the church. (We'll further discuss this passage in the next chapter.)

Abruptly, Tony ended the premarital counseling session, saying he had to tend to "something unexpected." He said he'd phone soon to set up our second meeting. I knew such a meeting would never occur. The next day I received a message on my voice mail: "Reverend Al," Tony announced, "Ruth and I have decided to seek another clergy person to officiate our wedding." This was the last time I heard from Tony or Ruth.

The Tactic of Spiritual Alienation

Dr. Murray describes another common tactic used by teen boys against young women of faith: alienating young women from their faith communities. "Most of the girls I see who are from a religious background are Christian," Murray says. "They have gone to church with their parents every Sunday and have attended parochial school, their family has a very strong relationship with God, and their faith is a source of great comfort and strength."

Gradually, Dr. Murray says, an abusive boy may chip away at the core foundation of a Christian girl's belief system. "Suddenly, this guy enters the picture and, very slowly, he starts criticizing her faith," she explains. "He begins tempting her to not go to church or Sunday school because he wants to be with her, or he has some sort of catastrophe that comes up, say maybe at 7:00 Sunday morning, which precludes her from going to church with her family. She's not even allowed to attend church youth group any longer because of his demands and possessiveness. Or he accuses her of being attracted to boys in the youth group, or even having a thing for the pastor or priest. He creates all these things to make her feel guilty about something she loves, her Christian faith."

Female Subordination—Views from the Second-Class Pews

Historically, the Christian church has placed females in a subordinate position to males. Church teachings that have been especially damning to girls and women center on the alleged God-given authority men have over women. Whether or not it is the intent of those Christian clergy and lay people who espouse such a patriarchal construct, we must all take heed of the fact that boys and men use this so-called "divine privilege" to their advantage. Many girls and women are cursed, beaten, strangled, and raped by Christian males who have no fear of being held accountable by church members for their criminal behavior. After all, we are told, they are "men of God."

After subjecting his seventeen-year-old girlfriend, Sarah, to constant emotional, physical, and sexual torture, nineteen-year-old Lawrence, a Christian preparing to become a missionary, decided to break up with the young woman he had battered. "He said I was crazy and hysterical and I needed to find myself," Sarah recalls. "He also said I wasn't the person I once was and that God had something else that was better and bigger for him." The God talk was an ongoing tactic, Sarah says. "Throughout our relationship, Lawrence used God a lot to support his actions and views. He'd say, 'I was doing my devotions this morning, and thinking about this verse.' He'd spent more time in church, did more devotions, and wanted to talk with me about these things. But he'd never apologize for abusing me. I don't think that he thought there was anything wrong with how he was treating me."

The ill treatment Sarah received from Lawrence was not the first time someone used Christianity to hurt her. "In the Christian tradition in which I was raised," she says, "females didn't have a lot of rights—at home or in the church. We weren't able to participate in or make certain decisions in the home, like how and where money was spent. There were very few freedoms I had as a female." As a result, Sarah says her spirit was stifled. "I lived under entirely different rules than males," she says. "I didn't think God gave callings to women as much as to men. It seemed as though men were given opportunities to pursue callings in business, music, etc. Doors would open to men as if this was something God was guiding them to do. In my view, women were not given the same opportunities." Asked if she internalized the message of subordination, Sarah replied, "Definitely. My church traditions gave me the message that there were certain things females could and could not do. Therefore, growing up, I often took the role of being submissive."

Dr. Jill Murray sees many young Christian women in her practice. "Spiritually, girls are given the message that they are somehow lesser than boys," she says. "Girls are told they should be subservient to boys, and males are to dominate females in whatever way they choose. This I would consider spiritual abuse."

Female Subordination—The Message from the Pulpit
Female subordination is held firmly in place by both the leadership style of some Christian male pastors and also by the manner in which these pastors present this doctrine from the pulpit. When Christian male leaders categorize females as delicate or sexualized objects, or as subservient beings needing males to "complete" or to "protect" them, then females are more likely to accept this subjugated role as God's will for their lives. When females hear Christian male pastors proclaiming from the pulpit that God commands girls and women to graciously honor, obey, serve, and submit to the alleged "God-ordained" authority males possess, it becomes very difficult for females to accept their own God-given power and authority.

Niki Christiansen is troubled over how the church contributes to the subordination of females, even those women in leadership positions. "We constantly have to fight messages that place us in the role of being submissive," says the long-time Christian and youth pastor serving at West Court Street Church of God in Flint, Michigan. According to Christiansen, the messages are often subtle. "Even when blatant statements aren't being made," she says, "the church still operates in a male entitlement mode. Within Christianity itself, women are said to be the 'gentle sex' and the 'weaker sex.' Ultimately, these descriptions translate into women not receiving the same rights and respect as men. There's no sense of equality within the church."

Christiansen cites as an example the fact that men fill most key church positions. "Leadership roles that tend to have more spiritual responsibilities are usually offered to men," she says. "Whether the position is chair of the church council or board of trustee member, as people of faith, we still think that somehow men can do these jobs better. When a nominating committee is asked to present people for consideration, they usually suggest men. The main exception to this rule is when the position is in Christian education. This feeds the stereotype that says, within church leadership, women can have authority only with children."

God's Intention

God and Jesus Christ never intended for Christian beliefs, teachings, and traditions to cause discrimination, suffering, or death to people, female or male. However, throughout history men have used these tenets to justify their violation of women and children. The practice continues to this day.

The patriarchal system has certainly always been alive and well in Christianity. Both the Hebrew Bible and Christian Scripture have an androcentric, or male-centered, perspective and emerge from patriarchal societies. Some texts, which actually are misogynist (women-hating), are lifted up to the exclusion of other texts that clearly affirm mutual respect between the sexes. Still other texts have been twisted—inadvertently and intentionally—to suggest that our loving and merciful God and Jesus Christ for some reason grant males authority and privilege over females. Because of all the above, men have received special dispensation from Christian clergy and laity alike to do whatever they desire with their wives, girlfriends, daughters, and all other females, without any fear of accountability.[1] The subordination of girls and women by boys and men—especially when male Christians use this to abuse females verbally, emotionally, physically, sexually, and spiritually—is both blasphemous and desecrating. Placing girls and women in subservient positions at church, home, or in the community is also an affront to the divine. God and Jesus Christ bestow equal value upon all human beings. Ultimately, the subjugation of females by males also imprisons boys and men. We will never be free to realize the full breath and depth of our humanity if we continue to deny girls and women their equal power and value, which is bestowed by God.

Popular Culture—A 21st Century Assault

How does popular culture influence the way teens view themselves as young adults? What are some of the messages that inform their social views on sexuality, dating, and intimate partner violence? We will devote the rest of this chapter to exploring these important questions.

Teen Sexuality: "Hooking Up" with a Wildfire

An eighteen-year-old female fashion model introduced me to a contemporary definition of the phrase "hooking up" while we were flying as seat mates from Honolulu to Los Angeles. Our five-hour conversation began shortly after take-off when, unsolicited, she started showing me a number of popular international magazine covers on which she was featured. It was a virtual global tour of some of the most exotic spots on Earth. However, there was a very troubling side to our conversation: At every photo shoot—whether in a sprawling metropolis, tiny alpine village, or on the sands of a remote Polynesian island—the young woman had engaged in what appeared to be an endless array of one-night stands.

Without hesitation, she spoke openly about "hooking up" with Phil and Jack and Ted and Mike and Carl and Leo and Vince and Steve and Paul and Harold. "All great gentlemen," was how the model described these men, though she quickly added she'd not be "hooking up" with any of them again because of "complicated circumstances." I took the latter phrase to mean the men were probably involved with other intimate partners.

Paternally, I mentioned to the young woman that I hoped she was maintaining healthy boundaries with the men to avoid getting hurt emotionally, physically, and spiritually. (Just having met, I did not feel comfortable coming right out and saying that I hoped she was practicing safe sex.) The euphemistic approach, it turns out, was all that was needed. "It's really sweet of you, sir, to be concerned about my safety," she said. "However, hooking up is about having a casual, carefree and wonderful time; it's not about having sex." There was something in her explanation that caused me to still worry about the well-being of this eighteen-year-old. And, as our flight continued to speed across the Pacific, I soon discovered why this was the case.

"Sure, there's plenty of passion when I hook up with a guy," she confessed later, "you know, kissing and all that kind of stuff. But it's totally safe." Not true. Before our flight touched down in Los Angeles, the woman had freely disclosed engaging in both anal and oral sex with every man she "hooked up" with during her worldwide modeling gig. Furthermore, as I had suspected, the "complicated circumstance" that precluded her from "hooking up" with these men again was that all of them had other female intimate partners, wives, or girlfriends. Thus, not only was the young woman placing herself at high risk for contracting a sexually transmitted disease, but all the "great gentlemen" she met at every port of call had reduced her to nothing more than a beautiful piece of meat.

As disturbing as my five-hour conversation was with the eighteen-year-old model, I'm more troubled over the fact that her situation is in no way rare. Across the United States, teen boys and teen girls are engaging in risky sexual activity with little regard for their emotional, physical, or spiritual safety and well-being.

"I don't think kids are educated enough to know the risk of sexually transmitted diseases, and how easy it is to get pregnant," says seventeen-year-old Vanessa Silver, a senior at Phoenix High School in Norco, California. Trained by her school counselor in a program called Conflict Mediation, Vanessa helps other students deal with various problems teens face. "If teens were more educated about the risks, I don't think as many would be involved in sexual activity. It seems that nowadays fewer and fewer people are virgins." Asked to elaborate on the kinds of sexual activity she hears about Vanessa responds, "I'm talking about sexual intercourse; the women themselves are telling me this."

Dr. Jill Murray also is seeing a disturbing trend in sexual activity among adolescents and even younger. "The popular culture that kids are living in now is very, very sexualized," she says. "I'm finding more and more, in both my private practice and presentations, that sexual intercourse is occurring at younger and younger ages. I'm currently seeing a twelve-year-old girl who's pregnant. I'm also currently seeing a thirteen-year-old boy who has impregnated his twelve-and-a-half-year-old girlfriend. I mean, these are girls who have had one or two or three menstrual cycles, and now they're pregnant."

Intercourse is only one of many sexual activities in which teens are involved. In order to prevent pregnancy, remain a virgin (at least, in their minds), and to avoid (they think) contracting a sexually transmitted disease (STD), young men and young women engage in anal sex, oral sex, mutual masturbation, and outercourse (explained below). Although most teens would categorize these behaviors as "safe," each activity poses its own risk.

Meg Meeker is a physician practicing pediatrics and adolescent medicine in Traverse City, Michigan. She is also a popular speaker on teen issues, and is the author of *Epidemic: How Teen Sex Is Killing Our Kids* (Washington, D.C.: Life-Line Press, 2002). Dr. Meeker describes the dangers associated with alleged "safe sex" activities:

> Teens are smart when it comes to figuring out how not to break the rules but how to come as close as possible. The "rules" when it comes to sex are maintaining your virginity and not getting pregnant or sick. So in addition to oral sex, they've integrated mutual masturbation, outercourse, and anal sex into their sexual repertoire.
>
> Mutual masturbation involves teens who fondle one another's genitalia, sometimes to the point of orgasm, sometimes not. It can range anywhere from soft petting to aggressive, full masturbation. Mutual masturbation may seem like a "safe" way for kids to have sex, but any time body fluids are exchanged, there's a risk of disease.
>
> Outercourse, another form of supposedly safe sex, is similar to mutual masturbation and, in fact, may include it. It usually involves intense rubbing of the genitals against a partner's body with clothes on or off, sometimes resulting in orgasm. Often a teenage boy will ejaculate near his partner's vagina but outside of it, perhaps on her stomach or thigh.
>
> These two techniques might sound safe enough— after all, at least they're not having actual intercourse. But any time genitalia come in contact with another person—

whether it's that person's hands, mouth, or body—there is the potential for transmission of an STD. And one form of seemingly safe sexual behavior can lead very easily to a less safe form. Outercourse, for example, often leads to intercourse.

Teens who are in a relationship with a boyfriend or girlfriend and fear pregnancy will experiment with ways to sexually satisfy each other. They will start one activity, such as mutual masturbation or outercourse, but when their arousal takes over, they switch to another—often intercourse. Let's face it, once kids hit the intensity of mutual masturbation or outercourse, trying to turn back from real intercourse is like trying to throw a car into reverse while it's going seventy miles an hour down the freeway.[2]

In addition to the risk of contracting an STD or conceiving an unwanted pregnancy, teens involved in sexual activities are in great danger of feeling degraded and of losing the gift of true intimacy. For example, let's look back for a moment at the story told earlier in the chapter about the eighteen-year-old fashion model. There was nothing in her description of the ongoing one-night stands she had with married or other unavailable men that seemed either intimate or respectful. In fact, the so-called "great gentlemen" with whom she had anal and oral sex reduced her from an intelligent, feeling, and lovely person to an ultimately easily discarded object.

"For many teens, sex isn't anything sacred, anything intimate, anything personal, or anything involving a loving interaction; sex is just bodies having sex," says Dr. Jill Murray. "Oral sex is so common that it's not even looked at twice. And, for teen girls, this is a way they can still feel like they're virgins. They feel like they can't get any diseases, which, of course, is untrue. And the girls know oral sex won't cause pregnancy. But many of these same girls end up feeling demeaned because, in spite of the fact that boys say they'll respect the girls even more after oral sex is performed—which is another manipulative tactic teen males use—they don't respect the girls at all. The boys simply move on to other girls they can use."

I once asked twelve high-school seniors, females and males, to confidentially write down their description of intimacy in a dating relationship. Here are their responses:

- French kissing
- showering together
- going "down" on a guy (oral sex)
- getting a "domer" from a girl (oral sex)
- "booty duty" (anal sex)
- lying naked together in bed
- having a guy give me a "hot, white pearl necklace" (when a boy ejaculates on her upper torso)
- giving a girl a "rim shot" (when a boy ejaculates near the girl's vagina)
- getting each other "off" (mutual masturbation)
- walking on the beach together
- "studding my stud" (girl performing oral sex on a guy with metal pierced in her tongue)

These descriptions of intimacy are very physical, almost mechanical, and include few references to emotions, feelings, or to a teen being seen or "known" by her or his partner.

Sexuality is not the only area in which young adults have been influenced by modern society. The way teens feel and think about themselves and other people, in and outside of dating relationships, has also been directly affected by popular culture. Below, a teen dating-violence survivor, a seventeen-year-old high school senior, an educator who works primarily with teen males, a mother of a fifteen-year-old abusive son, and a Christian pastor serving children and families all share their perspectives on this issue.

Teen Self-Esteem: Developing Images of Self and Others

"I Don't Look Like Anyone on MTV": Amy's Story II
Amy Woods says she received mixed messages from various segments of society about growing up female. "As far as my family goes, they were extremely supportive," says the twenty-two-year-old survivor of an abusive boyfriend, whom she dated when they were both teens. "I was raised in a Catholic Christian home, with those beliefs about self-respect, sexual purity, and placing equal value on all humanity. My mom and dad always told me, 'Amy, you can be whatever you want to be; you can achieve anything you want to achieve; we're here to help you.'"

The messages Amy received from popular culture about being female had a less positive impact. "As a pre-teen, I was very much a tomboy, whatever that stereotype represents," she says. "I had short hair; I was always out talking dirty. But right after I hit puberty, when my body started to change, I began paying more attention to music, MTV, and movies. I remember questioning my looks and feeling like I was ugly. I was short and stocky while all the other girls in my class seemed to be tall and bone thin. I just remember feeling unattractive. And, of course, I'd tell myself, 'I don't look like anyone on MTV.' This devastated me even more."

Amy recalls feeling torn between remaining true to her independent and unique self, and conforming to the messages of popular culture. She chose to try to conform. "I never wore make-up in high school," she says. "But I began wondering if I should, because all the other girls were wearing it, and I wanted to fit in. So I began to get the latest styles in clothing and shoes. Still, I remember hearing the word 'feminine' and feeling that this didn't describe me. In my own terms, I felt 'butch.'"

Describing the negative impact of not fitting into the stereotype of what popular culture defined as feminine Amy said, "I just remember doubting myself immensely. My girl-friends were all thin and beautiful—with nice skin. I didn't look at all like them. This really ate away at me. My self-esteem was taken down a lot."

"Women Should Be Viewed As People, Not as Objects": Rachel DeYoung

Seventeen-year-old Rachel DeYoung of Minneapolis takes issue with the many ways she witnesses popular culture marginalizing females. She even takes issue with this author when asked during our interview how she thinks women should be viewed in today's society. "We should be viewed as people, and not as objects," she said. "And, by the way, people don't generally ask how a man should be viewed. I think you should get to the point that this question will never be asked of a woman."

She is particularly troubled by all the negative images of females portrayed in films, videos, and television. Planning to become a screenwriter and documentary filmmaker, Rachel hopes to change people's perceptions of women. "There are so many movies out that are nothing but fluff," she says, "products produced solely to make money. I hope that everything I create will achieve a level of social consciousness instead of being the pointless endeavors currently being produced showing women in a negative light."

Many would assert that what we hear and see has no negative effect upon us. Rachel strongly disagrees. "People claim they are not affected by all the negativity currently out," she says, "but, to me, this seems completely untrue. Look at guys who listen to music or watch movies that are derogatory toward woman, then look at how those same guys treat woman. It's clear that these guys are being negatively influenced in their everyday lives by the media."

"Most Guys Genuinely Want the Same Things as Women": Daryl Bonilla

Daryl Bonilla admits to having an "edge" with young men when it comes to talking with them about teen dating violence issues. He's twenty-nine years old, still close enough to their age for them to describe Daryl as "cool." In addition, Daryl is an actor, born and raised in Hawaii, who has appeared in movies and television commercials the teens enjoy. "When I enter their classrooms, many teens will ask 'Aren't you the guy from the Bank of Hawaii commercial, and from the movie *Beyond Paradise*?'" Daryl says. "When I tell them I'm the same guy, the teens are at least open to hear what I have to say; they give me the benefit of the doubt."

Among his many responsibilities, Daryl works as the male educator for the Domestic Violence Clearinghouse and Legal Hotline in Honolulu. He and his colleagues speak to about two hundred young adults each month. Daryl has helped the agency develop curricula for all-male and all-female classrooms, as well as mixed-gender groups. "The material we write and present incorporates drama—exercises, scenarios, skits—into the programs to make our talks on teen dating violence awareness more interactive," he says.

"I think most guys genuinely want the same thing as women," Daryl says, "a loving and trusting relationship. But they often don't express this, because society says that as men they're not supposed to. In one of the workshops we do that deals with what men and women want, we've developed an exercise in which the students write down anonymously the top three things they want in an intimate relationship. We then compare what men want with what women want. Most often, everyone wants the same things: honesty, respect, trust. But, men and women would never know this because we're too busy assuming."

Daryl is especially troubled by the way males have bought into the acceptability of degrading females, popularized by various aspects of the media. "Derogatory and negative terms are being used by men to describe women in such a nonchalant manner in today's culture," he says. "When I'm walking down the halls of a high school, for example, on my way to do a presentation, I hear males referring to females as 'bitch,' 'ho,' 'slut,' 'skank,' and 'tuna,' a local term referring to a girl who is promiscuous. Not only do guys call women these derogatory terms, women call other women the same terms as well. Modern day society would have us believe that these words are cool. In reality, they are demoralizing females."

"Some Movies, Videos, and Music Recordings Are Designed to Keep Females in a Place of Inferiority": Florence's Story

Florence, a forty-seven-year-old Christian single mother with two teenage children, often wonders why she and her son, Jacob, have such a strained relationship. "I actually try to analyze it on a daily basis," she says. "We do relate, but it's not really mother-and-son-type of relating. And I'm really not sure why."

She remembers a time when things were better, long ago. "As a child, Jacob was really a pacifist," recalls Florence. "He sounded congenial, and I never had any problems with his friends. They never physically fought or argued. My son was a very socially adjusted boy." Then, when Jacob was eleven, things abruptly changed. He began listening to songs on the radio that degraded females. "The lyrics referred to women as 'bitches' and 'hos' and 'sluts,'" Florence explains. "At the time, Jacob and many of the other kids his age didn't know how offensive this language is to females. They were simply following the beat of the music. But, I think, the words were imprinted in their brains."

As Jacob got older, Florence says, he began to understand the degrading nature of the words, and used them against her. "I'd take offense if anybody referred to me as a 'bitch,'" Florence admits. "But when my own son started calling me a 'bitch' and 'slut,' I not only took offense, but was also very hurt. Jacob learned this vile behavior from the music he'd listen to, and also from movies, television, and videos." Florence disclosed that her son also has on occasion destroyed some of her property and threatened her with further violence. "Jacob has thrown dishes at me, yanked phone cords out of their socket, and has told me 'I'm going to kick your ass' and 'I'm going to kick your face.'" The anguished Christian mother identifies the media as one of the negative influences on her son. "Some movies, videos, and music recordings are designed to keep females in a place of inferiority," Florence says. "This is the exact position some males want women to remain in forever."

"A Culture at Odds with the Best Interest of Teens": Pastor Rick Roberts

"The prevalent messages that kids receive in today's culture is at odds with what truly is in the best health and interest of teens," Pastor Rick says. "What kids see in the media, what they hear from their peers, promotes negative role models. Boys do not have respect for girls and girls are trained to not even expect respect from boys." Pastor Rick describes some of the dynamics that create a negative relationship. "It's one where one member and, in my experience, that's usually been a male, is taking advantage of the dating partner emotionally and physically. And the dating partner might not even realize the behavior toward them is inappropriate; they may even believe it's normal." Reflecting spiritually on the self-esteem of young men and women, Pastor Rick says, "All teens, including those who are Christians, have challenges. Some of these struggles will, ultimately, lead them down very negative roads. But, if youth understand that they are valuable in God's eyes, then, hopefully, this will help give them the self-esteem to travel along a healthy path."

Conclusion

Christian teachings and popular culture have often done a disservice to young women and men. Facing such monumental challenges as trying to deal with their sexuality, some Christian leaders and parents tell teens simply to "remain both sexually abstinent and sexually pure to avoid danger." While the preceding statement may be true in some instances, it is not one that's very realistic. (Remember, Christian kids have the same hormones as do non-Christian kids!) Some Christian leaders and parents try to avoid the topic of teen sexuality altogether. Our lack of addressing the topic in a comprehensive and direct fashion creates a void that teens fill by popular culture, through movies, music, and other media. Their messages—"If it feels good do it," "Sexually active kids are popular kids," "Sex is not really sex unless you're having intercourse," and "You can't get hurt emotionally or physically if you don't have intercourse"— give teens a dangerous and distorted view.

Do we as church leaders and parents really want our daughters and sons to take their cues about human sexuality and intimacy from what they see on television and movies, or hear in popular music? Are we willing to continue avoiding the truth by denying that many of our own teens—even those raised in Christian homes—are engaged in risky sexual activity and unhealthy dating relationships? How will we choose to respond to these frightening, real-life issues?

Questions for Discussion

1. Why do you think many Christians choose to avoid the subject of teen sexuality?

2. If you are the parent of a teenage daughter or son, do you speak openly with him or her about their sexuality? If yes, what exactly do you discuss? If no, tell why you prefer not to address the subject.

3. Does your church and family teach that females and males have equal power and value? If yes, what exactly is taught? If no, describe what the church teaches about females and males.

4. What are four of the most negative messages popular culture gives to young women and men? Is your son or daughter embracing any of these messages? Be specific.

5. As a result of reading this chapter, what will you do differently as a parent or pastor to address teen sexuality, the subordination of females, and the influence of popular culture upon young men and women?

3.

Unique Challenges: Dating Violence among Urban African American Teens

An African American Young Man Steps Up

Eighteen-year-old Akijuwon Greene spent the first sixteen years of his life living in two different American inner cities. "I was born in Brooklyn, New York, and lived in Newark, New Jersey, for eight years," he says. "Then I moved to the South Bronx for three years. And now, for the past two years, I've lived in the suburbs, in the Pocono Mountains."

A senior at East Stroudsburg North High School in Bushkill, Pennsylvania, Akijuwon was raised in a dual religion family. "My mother is Christian and my father is Muslim," he explains. "What I received while growing up from the Christian Word was a message of peace and community. Jesus himself fed all the people who were hungry, and he healed those who were lame and sick. So, no matter what the preacher man would say about hell, I always thought the Christian message was about peace and service to the community."

Akijuwon says his Muslim roots are a lot more radical. "The Muslim part of me that I appreciate and from which I have learned the most taught me to be knowledgeable. This involved studying all kinds of things. I was a big fan of history when I was younger. So I've read a number of books about the past. This has helped me to get into activism."

As an activist, Akijuwon focuses much of his attention on ending the violence that young men perpetrate against young women in intimate relationships. "I've never witnessed first-hand a man physically abusing a woman," he admits. "But, both in the inner city and the suburbs, I've seen young men use mental abuse against young ladies." He cites as an example the repugnant behaviors some male teens have chosen when they didn't get what they've wanted from females. "I've witnessed guys spitting on girls and cursing them out with terms like 'bitch,' 'slut,' and 'ho,' simply because the young ladies didn't respond positively to the catcalls and whistles the guys were offering them. Personally, I think that this type of behavior always has been and always will be wrong. If I ever spit on anybody, or used such scathing terms to refer to a young lady, my mother would wring my neck. No matter what excuses anyone gives for such behavior, it's always wrong to use these tactics on any human being."

A year ago, Akijuwon put his activism into practice by joining thirty other teens in a program called Students Together for Outreach and Prevention of Abuse, or STOP Abuse. Founded by a domestic violence service agency, Women's Resources of Monroe County, Pennsylvania, STOP Abuse has the following goals:

- Provide information to teens, male and female, about the severity of the problem of sexual and domestic violence within their peer group
- Inform students about their rights and responsibilities relevant to these issues
- Dispel myths and stereotypes about sexual assault and relationship violence
- Reduce risk of assault and increase understanding and support for victims

- Encourage victims to get help
- Bridge the gap between children and teens in crisis and crisis intervention service providers
- Empower students to take an active role in changing the way their peers and society in general view these issues
- Provide the necessary skills for teens to become peer educators
- Provide teens media and legislative training to further advocate with legislature to change local, state, and national laws to support victims, end the assault on women and children, and end domestic and sexual violence.

Lisa Brito Greene, Akijuwon's mother, is a youth outreach advocate and a crisis counselor at Women's Resources. Most of her time is spent working with STOP Abuse students. "We train the teens to go back to their peers and talk with them about domestic abuse, and relationship and sexual violence," Ms. Greene says. "We also train the teens to be activists, advocates, and peer-educators. So, in addition to talking with their peers, STOP Abuse members also advocate with lawmakers around issues relating to children and teens. The teens are activists in that they help work on some of these issues in a political arena, as well as fighting for their school to change policies, practices, and so forth."

The teens involved in STOP Abuse receive forty hours of direct training, Ms. Greene says. Then, as a follow-up, there is a training component built into their weekly meetings. "They receive additional training related to domestic and sexual violence, and on advocacy and activism," Ms. Greene explains.

Ms. Green reflects on why Akijuwon decided to join the struggle to end the violence males perpetrate against females. "I guess I bring the work home," she says. "I'm constantly talking about these issues. And because I speak in middle and high schools, Akijuwon was able to attend one of my sessions. He saw other teens doing things to work toward ending domestic, relationship, and sexual violence, and it really interested him. I've been doing activism for a long time, and he desires to do the same."

Akijuwon himself says that he can no longer look the other way when confronted by the harsh realities of teen dating violence and sexual assault. "I hate to have to admit it," he confesses, "but, in the past, I've found myself in many situations where I saw guys doing wrong and could have intervened. Instead, I just turned my head and looked the other way." He says that fear was a primary motivation for his choosing not to act. "Today, I regret my behavior because I know some good might have come if I had taken action. But, like most of us, I made my choice out of fear. I didn't know what would have happened to me had I acted. Therefore, many times, I've chosen not to tell guys to stop their bad behavior because I was afraid. As much as I hate to admit it, the inner city is violent."

Realizing that true activism requires speaking against injustice, even when faced with danger, Akijuwon says he can no longer remain silent. "If I'm going to help others stop sexual assault and dating violence among teens, I need to first stop turning my head away from these issues," he says. "A larger sense of community needs to be installed if we are going to deal with the problems. Therefore, I, too, have to be fully involved."

Unique Challenges

Dating violence among teens from all ethnic and racial groups exhibits certain similarities. However, African American teens face some unique challenges. In the remaining portion of this chapter, we'll explore how popular culture, hip-hop music, racism, sexism, social status, and teachings traditionally espoused by African American Christian leaders about the role of females and males have greatly influenced how young black women and black men view intimate dating relationships, sexuality, spirituality, and themselves. Our focus will be on African American youth in urban areas.

Popular Culture: Willful Myopia

If we were to use pop culture as the sole reflector of the character, integrity, and value of African American teens, these particular young adults would fare very poorly. If we consider all the work that artists working in all media are producing, we can see the full scope of positive contributions African Americans are making in society. However, the popular music recordings and videos, magazines, movies, and television news stories that garner the most attention are those that depict black youth in a negative light. African American young adults are primarily portrayed as alcohol and drug users, foul-mouthed, hypersexual, inarticulate, pistol-whipping, violent, and subhuman.

"Unfortunately, what seems to be the most common representation of black females in pop culture, specifically in music videos, is that of the hyper sexualized female," says Leah Aldridge. Since 1989, she has worked with the Los Angeles Commission on Assault Against Women (LACAAW). Currently, Ms. Aldridge serves as the associate director of that organization's Youth Violence Prevention, Policy and Training. In this capacity, she supervises the development, implementation, and direction of violence prevention programs for youth, their families, and community. The LACAAW team serves approximately five thousand youth each month, 14 percent of whom are African American.

Ms. Aldridge discusses how pop culture has marginalized both black and white females, but in different ways. "Images of white girls in pop culture overwhelmingly support the notion that thinner is better," she says. "As a result, correlations have been drawn between these images and the rise of eating disorders among adolescent white females. However, for black females the focus shifts: Their sexuality is used to sell pop culture, in this case, rap and hip-hop videos. When sex and a product are so closely linked, the impact on broader society is dramatic. Unfortunately, the overrepresentation of the hypersexualized black female shifts a cultural norm. Youth are being taught that female sexuality is a commodity. We are left with a generation of young people whose attitudes regarding sex are cavalier and casual. Sex sells and advertisers have used this strategy for years. For many black teens, sex is the predominant image that they are sold. The notion of sexuality as a precious gift that is to be protected and given to another under special circumstances is gone."

Popular culture has also done a great disservice to African American young men by most often portraying them as hyper masculine, hypersexual, and violent. Black young men are also frequently stereotyped as being in an adversarial role with African American women. "Unfortunately for many black males, these images reinforce myths and stereotypes that they may have regarding black females," says Ms. Aldridge. "In addition to the myth of the sexually insatiable female, which translates into 'all women on the street want you the way the girls in the videos do,' another often promoted stereotype is one of gold-digging females who only want a man for his bling-bling [money]. These images constantly throw hypersexualized females (sex) into the mix with hypermasculine males as represented by gold, cars, crystal, and diamonds (money). This reinforces in the minds of many young people the idea that relationships are based on an exchange of sex for money, thus rendering our youth to adopt the prescribed societal roles or attitudes of 'pimps' and 'hos.' For many of today's youth, relationships are seen as inherently adversarial and untrustworthy. What we should be promoting is healthy emotional, physical, intellectual, spiritual, as well as sexual development between them. But, is this entertaining?"

MEE (Motivational Educational Entertainment) Productions Inc., a Philadelphia-based organization that develops socially responsible, research-based communication strategies, performed an exhaustive study of black urban youth sexuality and the influence of media. The organization spent a year collecting data, including interviews with black urban young people ages sixteen to twenty from households with less than $25,000 in annual income. The study also included a literature review, expert interviews, more than forty focus groups, and a two thousand sample-size media consumption and lifestyle survey. The findings are published in the report *This Is My Reality: The Price of Sex*, accompanied by a video of the same name (MEE Productions, 2004).

Here are some of the alarming facts that the study uncovered:

- *"Old school" thinking about relationships has become irrelevant.* Those who used to be called girlfriends are now "wifeys" and females desired only for sex are called "shorties." Condoms are not used in ongoing relationships, but are considered more important in casual sex. On the increase are adult male/teen female relationships. More out in the open among black urban youth are young females who are having sex with other females. These encounters are not necessarily described as "lesbian," and, for the most part, seem to be taken in stride by youth.

- *Parents both contribute to and impede healthy sexuality.* Some parents are either too uninformed themselves or too embarrassed to give their children the kind of values and information which can help them make good choices related to sex. Yet, youth say parents still have credibility and wield influence, based both on what they say and what they do. They also report that some adults are just as much a problem (if not more) than a solution to teen sexuality issues. Some parents are too strict or judgmental; others, youth say, are trying to be as "young" as their children, acting out at youth house parties or competing with teens in the way they dress or in their own sexual behaviors.

- *Black females are valued by no one.* Not only do males not trust females, but overwhelmingly, girls reported that they do not even trust each other, a surprising departure from the traditional "sistahood." Males, and even some females, regularly use derogatory sexual terms such as "hoodrats," "hos," "bitches," and "runners" to describe women and girls.

- *Abstinence and marriage are not reality for black urban youth.* Instant gratification—sexually and otherwise—is key, because these youth see no future for themselves. Some have seen few successful relationships or marriages in action, and therefore have no model on which to pattern one.

- *Sex education is not meeting the needs of youth.* Many young people are engaging in sexual activity before health classes are in their curriculum; and when classes are offered, they are not comprehensive enough to help youth understand the complexities, emotional effects, and consequences of sex.

- *Communication is poor in youth relationships.* Like many adults, youth are not exhibiting meaningful and effective communication within their relationships. They don't talk about feelings and expectations, and very seldom discuss sexual and reproductive health issues, including condom use.

- *Healthcare is accessible but not user friendly.* Overwhelmingly, some form of medical insurance or free services covered the youth in this study. Many, however, shared experiences where they were shamed, disrespected, and hurt during visits to clinics, hospitals, and other healthcare sites. This could make them less likely to pursue sexual health services when needed.

- *Males desire female virgins.* Girls who don't "give it up" are males' top choices for long-term partners. Yet males pressure females to have sex. Giving in "too easily" could leave a female in danger of not being taken seriously as a potential long-term mate.

- *"Wish I woulda waited."* When asked if they would have made different decisions if they knew then what they know now, many youth said they wished they would have waited before becoming sexually active. They admitted that the sex itself wasn't all it was cracked up to be and that being in a sexual relationship is more complicated than they thought.[1]

Hip-hop Culture: Facts and Myths

Personally, I believe that "ho," "bitch," and "slut" are all scathing terms. For sure, the use of these words has been magnified nowadays through the fact that mainstream media is no longer truly censored. Someone in the media is not doing his or her job. "Bitch" is even being said on network TV and radio programs. So, words once said only in the dark corners of alleys are now being recited on public streets in the light of day. Some guys are even introducing their ladies by saying "This is my bitch." That's certainly not right. But, hip-hop didn't cause all this negative behavior; it's been around since the dawn of time.

—Akijuwon Green

Let's take a close look at hip-hop culture and the impact media has on the way African American young men and young women feel and think about one another and themselves. We'll give special attention to rap, the musical component of hip-hop culture.

Chic Smith is co-founder and vice president of Urban Think Tank, Inc., headquartered in Brooklyn. The agency is a nonpartisan, community-based home for a body of thinkers in the hip-hop generation. It is the first organization that analyzes and frames political, economic, and cultural issues, particularly those of concern to people of color, from the perspective of the hip-hop generation. Urban Think Tank uses a multi-media strategy to encourage an open dialogue and to influence public policy changes.

Ms. Smith explains that hip-hop culture is "an artistic state or an existence, and I mean artistic in its most primitive form—creative, innovative, imaginative." The process, according to Ms. Smith, is still unfolding. "I always say that hip-hop is an evolving existence," she explains, "because when you're creative you start out with one thing and, often times by the end of the process, there's something totally different. And, this existence is expressed in the same manner that other cultures are expressed, which is through shared values, styles, behaviors, language, traditions. But it centers on the artistic and creative state of existence."

Although in its earliest form hip-hop was developed and created by African American and Latino young people, it is now a global phenomenon. "Hip-hop defies the boundaries of age, class, race," Ms. Smith says. "People from various ethnicities and generations have adopted it."

Misconceptions about hip-hop culture mirror the stereotypes that many people harbor about African Americans in general, especially black youth. "Hip-hop has been publicly exploited so badly," Ms. Smith says. "The very mention of the phrase conjures up a whole plethora of negative connotations: The forty-ounce-drinking, baby-having, baby-making, weed-smoking, baggy-pants wearing degenerate, who is lazy and uneducated. These stereotypes are so irritating."

According to Ms. Smith, even some of the folks who identify themselves as "hip-hop heads" misunderstand this culture. "People see someone like myself, or my business partner, or so many other individuals around the country who don't have on baggy pants and they say 'You're not down with hip-hop,'" she says. "It's clear to me that these people don't know what hip-hop culture is all about. The baggy pants are not hip-hop culture, but prison culture. This came about from people having their belts taken away in prison. However, because there are so few places that are open to the teaching and/or discussion of hip-hop culture, this kind of misinformation is accepted and distributed as truth."

Rap Music and Videos: Impact on Violence Against Women
I do not think that rap songs and music videos cause African American young men to abuse African American young women. However, it is my firm belief that any song or music video (rap or otherwise) that depicts the degradation and dehumanization of females by males is damnable. Glorifying men's abuse of women through physical or sexual violence, stalking, or the emotional guttering of females by referring to them as "bitches," "cunts," "hos," "sluts," or "tramps" destroys the mind, personhood, and spirit of women, and normalizes the violence for both males and females.

Ultimately, the glamorization of misogyny in some rap songs and music videos has a negative effect on men as well as women. These types of inappropriate expressions make it difficult for African American youth to engage in healthy, trusting, and egalitarian intimate dating relationships.

"I'm not at all for censorship of music," Chic Smith says, "but I do believe in accountability for your artistic gifts—accountability to yourself, to your creator, your family, your community, the whole spectrum." Ms. Smith believes that rap is often unfairly singled out as the one kind of music that encourages men's violence against women. "The truth of the matter is that various forms of music have contributed to the issue," Ms. Smith says. "But because rap music is a subset of hip-hop culture, which embodies all of the negative connotations that I mentioned earlier, it's easy for the media, recipients of misinformation, and other haters to single out rap music as a contributing factor to violence against primarily teen girls, but teen guys as well." Ms. Smith points out that some country songs promote men's violence against their female intimate partners as normal. "But the media doesn't scrutinize country music, nor are the same kinds of questions [about men's violence against women] being asked about blues, punk, or rock music."

Still, Ms. Smith admits some rap music has indeed had a negative impact upon young African American men and women. "We have to own up to the damage we ourselves have done that has contributed to the violence," she says. "I say 'we' because I too am a member of the hip-hop community." Ms. Smith is especially troubled, she says, by the disrespectful names some African Americans call themselves and one another. She specifically identified "nigger," "bitch," "ho," and "pimp."

"When we call each other something other than our own names, then we have no problem disrespecting the next woman or the next man," she says. "The use of these terms shows a lack of knowledge. We have no clue what it took for someone to call us by our true names. I don't have the

firsthand experience of living through the civil rights movement. But, because its achievements have been passed on to
me, I have a level of respect for it. Therefore, if someone calls
me something other than Chic, they will get no response. It
could even be 'hey babe,' but they'd get no response. If you
want my attention, and desire to get to know me personally, you'll do that respectfully. That's how I carry myself. Not
because I'm better than anyone, but because I value the leg-
acy of self-respect the ancestors died to leave me and future
generations."

A number of rap artists write songs that promote healthy
dating relationships, positive community support, and the
value of spirituality. But few of these recordings receive airplay on radio or music-video broadcasts. "Unless you are
a connoisseur and have a real appreciation for the musical
component of the culture," Ms. Smith says," you won't hear
the recordings with these positive images because they are
not getting air time, and there are no videos."

Having worked at radio stations and record companies,
and having earned a master of arts in telecommunication
policy and black culture, Chic Smith offers an expert view on
the behind-the-scenes process of how recordings and videos are chosen for airplay. "The record companies determine,
approve, sanction, and, in many instances, even craft the lyri-
cal content of a song," she explains. "And the producers and
directors, in association with the record companies, plan the
videos. Many rap artists think they've come up with the idea
for a song or music video when, in reality, they've been clev-
erly manipulated for marketing purposes to keep the record
company in riches."

Cultural Teachings, Racism, Sexism, and Social Status

Debasing ideological constructions of black woman-
hood are often concretely actualized through institutional

responses to victim-survivors of male violence. The official agencies authorized by our society to respond to the needs of women, such as the police, courts, and hospitals, can function in this capacity. Church practices and clergy responses to women sometimes reproduce the same effect as well. Sometimes these barriers are even found within organizations whose primary goal is to provide services that treat women in a countercultural fashion, such as battered women's shelters or rape crisis hot lines. Steeped in ideological presuppositions that stereotype black women or deny them their right to occupy a victim-status, the actions and silent disregard of state and private community groups exacerbates women's trauma.[2]

—Traci C. West, *Wounds of the Spirit*

Cultural teachings, racism, sexism, and social status have tremendous impact on how African American women, young and old, respond to situations of male intimate partner violence. These dynamics also influence how various segments of society treat black female victims/survivors after someone makes a disclosure of abuse.

Dr. Beth Richie is professor and head of the Department of African American Studies at the University of Illinois at Chicago. She has worked with victimized black female teens and adults for several years. I asked Dr. Richie to compare the experience of abused black women to that of abused women from other ethnic and racial backgrounds.

"Certainly the most mundane understanding of what it feels like to be in an abusive relationship—abuse of power and control, fear and secrecy—are all common experiences," Dr. Richie says. "But different social positions, especially the position of marginalization, have a profound affect on not just the experience of the violence, but also the experience of communal, cultural, familial, and societal reactions to the violence. So, while the violence may be experienced similarly, the response of the family member, hospital emergency room physician, a police officer, or a neighbor will differ depending on the social position that a victimized woman must assume."

Dr. Richie also points out the risks of treating intimate partner violence among teens as a one-size-fits-all crime. "Among young people, the [intimate] relationship may not be a cohabiting one," she says. "Among young people, the person who's experiencing gender violence may not be able to utilize services without parental permission. Among young people, peers may have a different influence than in adult relationships. So, on every level, to design a prevention campaign, or an intervention strategy, or treatment protocol, or even an intake form, things need to be tailored to the particular experience of the population."

Dr. Richie says that the anti-violence movement needs to look at how other groups tailor their services to ensure no one is left out. "Alcoholics Anonymous meetings work differently in different communities," she says. "And, if you're designing a diet for people who are diabetic, you have to take into account the kind of food each person eats. In most other examples of trying to respond to a social problem to help people, we've appreciated that differences will matter. That appreciation hasn't happened as much in our movement as it needs to. One of the consequences of this is that we've left lots of people unprotected and outside of the realm of who we've identified as maybe even deserving of services."

Law Enforcement
The relationship between urban African Americans and law enforcement has historically been tense. Traci C. West, a United Methodist clergy member, writes in her book *Wounds of the Spirit* that much of this tension has to do with distrust. "Women's testimony about their distrust of the police or of state social workers, based on specific experiences and

'knowledge,' demonstrates the hidden, informal barriers that leave them feeling stranded and trapped. Their subjugated knowledge belies the established, formal label of state institutions that are supposed to serve and protect the public interest."[3]

Dr. Beth Richie echoes this sentiment. "Someone who is in a community with a high rate of police brutality will have a different reaction from her neighbor if she calls the police," Dr. Richie says. "She may also have a negative reaction from the police themselves, if and when they come. She may feel a sense of loyalty to the man who assaulted her and, therefore, may be hesitant to call the police at all. She may drop the charges altogether. She may have something illegal happening in her household, and thus calling the police around her victimization leads to the arrest of someone other than her offender. Each level of marginalization, if you will, brings with it lots of complications, over and over again, which lead to a multiple negative impact."

Comparing the abuse of African American teen and adult women with those females from other races, Dr. Richie observes the following. "So, the hit still hurts; the stab still cuts; the words still degrade; and, to add to all of this, other social circumstances, conditions, and reactions further complicate matters."

Loyalty

The sense of loyalty victimized teens and adult women feel for the men who abuse them is found in all ethnic, racial, and socioeconomic strata. Many factors account for this devotion. To name just a few:

- Cultural and religious teachings that co-opt women into believing they cause, and therefore must rectify, all the problems occurring in their intimate relationships with men

- Economic dependency (which is rarely the case in teen dating relationships)
- Emotional dependency (cultural and religious brainwashing that trick women into believing they are not "complete" without a man, and that "love conquers all" the problems couples face)
- Promises by the perpetrator to stop his abusive behavior and somehow become a "changed man"
- Threats by the perpetrator to harm himself or his female intimate partner if she leaves the relationship

The loyalty many African American and other marginalized women feel toward their male violators often involves additional complexities. Dr. Beth Richie explains: "There is a complicated relationship, I think, between various communities and law enforcement and other social institutions," she says. "The women who feel that these institutions have been hostile to them, to their community, and to members of their family may hesitate to use the institutions in responding to any problem of an intimate or interpersonal nature."

Focusing directly on loyalty in African American teens, Dr. Richie sought caution as not to overgeneralize. "I don't want to paint a kind of monolithic picture of black adolescents and sentiments about loyalty," she said. "But African American males have been labeled as the 'endangered species' in our community. And so to participate in further endangering them through protecting oneself can be a very complicated set of issues to negotiate as a young black woman who is experiencing victimization."

"I'm a Strong, Independent Black Woman!":
Encounter with Joan
Immediately following a keynote address I delivered on teen dating violence awareness, Joan approached me. She was a nineteen-year-old university freshman. For seven months

she had been dating a university sophomore, also black; let's call him Troy. The relationship started wonderfully, according to Joan. She and Troy biked, hiked, and studied African American history together. They loved to cook and laughed constantly at each other's jokes. But by the time Joan and I met, her relationship with Troy was no laughing matter.

"At times he can be really mean," was how Joan described her boyfriend's abusive behavior. Troy punched his girlfriend in her abdomen; forced her head into a toilet bowl, and twice put a hot iron against Joan's buttocks to help her "burn off some weight." He also often referred to Joan as a "stupid, good-for-nothing-but-a-fuck, lazy bitch."

After Joan disclosed her story, I told her no one deserves the emotional and physical torture Troy was inflicting on her. I was shocked by the response she offered. "Oh, Rev. Miles, don't worry about me," she said. "I'm a strong, independent black woman—not one of those victimized women you spoke about in your keynote address. I've hit Troy at times, too; we have always fought. Next time I'm going to be better prepared to do battle with him."

This story raises several critical issues. Let's consider two of these. First is the idea of an intimate dating partnership being likened to a war zone where one member, in this case Joan, must prepare to "do battle." Many urban African American youth did not grow up in homes where adults modeled healthy intimate partnerships. On the contrary, some were raised with no adult male present. Other black youth grew up in homes where the adult males either living in or visiting in the home abused their mothers, grandmothers, aunts, or older sisters. Thus, young women and young men learn their intimate dating practices from the unhealthy situations they watched their mothers go through, from their teen peers, or from the media.

The second critical issue needing further attention is the notion of a strong, independent black woman. As used by

Joan, and by several other African American female survivors of teen and adult intimate partner violence who have shared their stories with me, "strength" seems to be equated with endurance and a willingness to fight back. On the other hand, "weakness" is apparently indicated by seeking assistance rather than fighting back, or by attempting to get out of an abusive relationship.

"In a larger societal context white women may be perceived as 'weak' and black women as 'strong,'" says Leah Aldridge who works with the Los Angeles Commission on Assault Against Women (LACAAW). "This common perception may have originated from slavery. Black women worked the fields while white women sat in the shade, lest they be exposed to the sun. They needed black women to keep their houses and nurse their children. This was reinforced until the civil rights movement when black women walked miles during the bus boycotts to tend the homes of the 'helpless and dependent' white women. As a result of this history, the perception of white women as weak and black women as strong was a natural conclusion to draw." Ms. Aldridge further explains. "Historically, what is called domestic violence didn't happen in the black community." She discusses how African American women have generally categorized the violence men perpetrate against them and how they continue to contrast their situations with the abuse faced by white women.

"As women began to speak out about violence in their homes, publicly the voices had white faces attached to them. The image of a battered woman was one of a defeated, helpless, powerless white woman. In the minds of black women, we were too strong to be battered. Black couples had 'fights' and it just so happened that the men always won these 'fights.' Consequently, many black women were not taught to identify and heed the warning signs of domestic violence, were not taught that violence in relationships is wrong, were not taught that no one deserves to be abused, and we were not taught that it's okay to end an abusive relationship. The message many of us were taught by our mothers and grandmothers was: 'Don't let any man put his hand on you. If he does, you pick up a brick, a skillet, a knife, and you take him out.' The unspoken message was 'it's okay to stay in the relationship, just beat his ass before he beats yours!'"

Ms. Aldridge is concerned that these messages tend to have an intergenerational impact on intimate partner violence among African Americans.

"We are not being taught that there is a better way, there's another way, or there's a healthier way to relate to each other," she says. "And so, we pass on those negative messages, typically from our mothers and grandmothers, out of their own life experience. Thus, many black teenage girls come into an intimate relationship on edge, ready to fight. They tell black brothers, 'Look, if you ever put your hands on me, I'm going to kick your ass.' Now, is that a healthy way to start a new relationship?"

According to Ms. Aldridge, black people must take better caution regarding the kinds of messages we pass on to our daughters and sons. "African American culture is not inherently violent, although racist attitudes would suggest otherwise," she says. "But without serious interventions on individual, familial, communal, societal, and spiritual levels to change the social norm that compels black women to endure interpersonal violence as a test of our strength, tolerance for violence will remain the norm in many African American relationships."

African American Christian Teachings: Harmful or Helpful?

Over the years, a lot of abused women, most of them African Americans, have told me the first place they turned for help was the church. What's interesting is the fact that they've felt a lack of support, especially from male Christian leaders. The women who went to their male ministers said they were told to 'go back home and be a better wife.' This type of counsel makes it seem as though the abuse was the woman's fault. I've also been around male Christian ministers who believe we should treat women in the same way we treat a child. So, by definition, the contributions of women in church and society are looked upon by some Christian ministers as less than those of men.

—Dr. Oliver J. Williams, executive director of the Institute on Domestic Violence in the African American Community, St. Paul, Minnesota

History provides irrefutable evidence on how the African American church and its leaders have championed such moral and social concerns as working to bring an end to racism and poverty. Black Christians have spoken out boldly against these societal ills, even in the face of beatings, castrations, incarcerations, rapes, murders, lynching, and other evils perpetrated by white males.

However, in terms of working toward ending men's violence against women, black male clergy and male lay leaders have, for the most part, not been helpful, and have even been hurtful. This is especially the case when the batterer himself is a church member. Two reasons for the lack of involvement are misogyny and patriarchy. Both practices lead male Christian clergy and laity to collude with, or to excuse and justify, the abuse Christian men inflict upon their wives and girlfriends. Misogyny and patriarchy also compel male clergy and laity to blame women. Let's take a closer look at both practices.

We are concentrating here on male African American clergy and lay leaders, because this chapter is focused on intimate partner violence among urban black teens. Misogyny and patriarchy is as big a problem among male clergy and lay leaders from all other ethnic and racial backgrounds. In terms of white male clergy and lay leaders, the problems are even greater because these men have the full benefit of male privilege.

Misogyny: We Must Take a Stand!

One afternoon, just prior to leaving my office to travel to the U.S. mainland to conduct a two-day clergy conference on domestic violence in the African American community, I received a frantic phone call from the conference organizer, a female clergy member. She informed me that the teenage son of the head of their African American ministerial alliance, which was made up of twenty black male clergy and the black female conference organizer, had just been arrested the night before for physically and sexually assaulting his girlfriend. The young man confessed his crimes to the arresting law enforcement officers, the female clergy member told me. But the young man made it clear that his actions were caused by the young woman "provoking" him and flirting with other guys.

The reason the conference organizer had decided to phone me, I learned, was because at an emergency meeting of the ministerial alliance that same afternoon, all the male clergy members had decided to get involved. "We must take a stand!" was what they told one another. Their response to the young man's confessed crimes did not include holding him accountable for the sinful and unlawful attacks he perpetrated against his girlfriend or making sure he got into batterers' treatment or offender-specific counseling to help him stop his violent behavior; nor did they plan to urge the young man to apologize to the woman he victimized and pay her restitution.

Instead, the "stand" taken by these Christian men of God was to go to court with the offending young man and demand that the judge set him free immediately.

During my time in their city, the twenty African American male clergy of the ministerial alliance sought my consultation on this case by setting up a two-hour private session with me. At one point during our time together, I asked the spiritual leaders why they so readily chose to help the young abusive man escape justice. The question was met with dead silence. Finally, one clergy member said, "Women are such tramps, sleeping around on and trying to ruin fine black men. This young lady provoked [the young man] to attack her. She ought to be in jail, not him." Not one clergy member spoke against this particular pastor's blatant misogyny. Subsequently, the male African American teenager who admitted to physically and sexually assaulting his girlfriend was freed of both charges.

Patriarchy

Patriarchal teachings are a major part of African American Christian culture. In a number of black churches, only males can hold such key positions as bishop, board member, choir director, deacon, elder, treasurer, and pastor. The Hebrew Bible, Christian Scripture, God, and Jesus Christ are all used to demonstrate that males have special divine favor.

For example, proponents of the hierarchical view of the sexes usually draw on only one of the creation stories to support their view. They cite only Genesis 2:18-25, which depicts woman's creation from man's rib. They don't mention a parallel account of the creation of woman and man in Genesis 1:26-27: "Then God said, 'Let us make humankind in our image, according to our likeness; and let them have dominion over the fish of the sea, and over the birds of the air, and over the cattle, and over all the wild animals of the earth, and over every creeping thing that creeps upon the earth.' So God created humankind in his image, in the image of God he created them; male and female he created them" (NRSV).[4] The verses from the Christian Scriptures most frequently cited to justify men's authority over women are Ephesians 5:21-33. Although the book's author offers guidelines for both husbands and wives worshiping near the city of Ephesus, over the centuries these passages have been used to elevate the status of men and put women down. Seldom do clergy members or congregants discuss the fact that nine of the twelve verses carry instructions for Christian husbands to follow. An inordinate amount of attention has been paid to what these verses tell wives, rather than what they demand of men. The passages clearly instruct husbands to love their wives as they do their own bodies. Nevertheless, the verses are often used to instruct women on what they are to do for their husbands—even those husbands who abuse their wives.[5] For further insights into these biblical passages, read the sermon, "Qualities of a Healthy Christian Marriage," in Appendix A.

Females, we are told, are less than males. Many African American church circles teach that the highest calling women can achieve is to serve Christian men—husbands, pastors, and all others.

Rev. Traci C. West addresses this issue in *Wounds of the Spirit:*

> Churches represent a community resource that should offer women coping with the crisis of male violence a caring response. Unfortunately, church practices and leaders too often neglect or dismiss the needs of women who have been victimized. Such behavior reinforces social mores that assume that black women are, and ought to be, resilient, sacrificing, persevering martyrs in spite of such "trials." Sometimes the neglect is manifested in the tremendous demands that the "work ethic" of internal church culture places on its women members. This ethic is usually indifferent to the issues of male violence that women face

and privately discuss with the pastor, in women's prayer groups, or informally with church friends. Of course, victim-survivors need to have confidential resources available to them, both informal and pastoral. Yet "secrets" about abusive husbands and fathers can become common knowledge within congregations, while failing to provoke any action to stop the violence. Meanwhile, endless cooking and serving for fund-raisers, planning for revivals, arranging for bus trips, and organizing the church school remain the unaltered, energy-consuming agenda for church women.

No matter how many instances of male violence are confided to the pastoral staff or raised in the women's prayer group, the institutional priorities of the church seldom shift toward offering women a supportive and empowering response. At the same time, when Christian teachings that appear to sanction male violence in the home by advocating patriarchal authority over women and children remain unchallenged, the church environment functions as an incubator of abuse and a purveyor of the exploitative treatment of women.[6]

Patriarchal constructs, which generally have the full blessing of male African American clergy and church lay leaders, make it easy for black men and boys to do whatever they please with black women and girls without any concern for being held accountable for their abusive behavior (as attested to by the story told earlier in this chapter). Male-centered teachings also set up an imbalance in female-male intimate partnerships, both dating and marital, making it very difficult, if not impossible, for African American females and males to share the joy of a mutually healthy, mutually loving, mutually respectful intimate relationship that is fully equal in all respects.

Conclusion

African American youth living in urban areas face unique challenges in dating relationships. While some of these young adults have grown up in homes with both fathers and mothers who treat each other, and their children, with love and respect, many black youth have been raised in environments where the adult couple has been adversarial toward each other, or the adult male has been abusive to his female intimate partner and her children, or there has been no adult male consistently present in the home. As a result, many black teens have not received proper modeling on what constitutes a healthy dating relationship. The young women and men have had to turn to their peers or to various segments of popular culture, especially the media, for guidance.

Hip-hop music and videos, to which many urban African American youth subscribe, pose yet another challenge. Although a number of rap artists create healthy and positive work, the songs and music videos receiving the most air time and viewership are those that stereotype black males as hypermasculine and hypersexual, and cast black females in degrading and hypersexualized positions.

The African American church and its male leaders have also been harmful. Many black male clergy and lay leaders teach doctrine that is misogynic and patriarchal in nature. Adhering to these constructs sets an imbalance between women and men, causing females to feel subjugated to males in and outside of intimate relationships. The teachings also send the message to males that they can do to females whatever they choose to and be excused and justified by both church and society.

The challenges urban African American youth face are both unique and overwhelming, but not irrevocable. If parents and pastors are to help those young people who are at risk, we must first examine, and then be willing to change, our own beliefs and attitudes that keep both young black men and black women from living their lives in the healthy fashion God intends for all humans.

Questions for Discussion

1. What are three of the challenges African American youth face in dating relationships? How are you responding to these particular situations?

2. Are there African American youth in your community or church involved in teen dating violence? What is your church and community doing to deal with these matters?

3. How do you feel about the way African American youth are being portrayed in movies and music videos? Please elaborate.

4. What actions constitute violence in an intimate-partner relationship? If you think violence may be acceptable in certain situations, explain your position. If you believe violence is never acceptable, explain your position.

5. In your Christian church, are females and males being treated as equals? If yes, please give specific examples of this equality. If no, tell why equal power and values of males and females are not being taught.

6. As a result of reading this chapter, how, if at all, will your response to and views of teen dating violence among African American youth change?

4.

How Clergy, Youth Ministers, Christian Educators, and Parents Can Help

My parents would question and always identify the marks on my body. They'd say "I don't believe you" when I offered my excuses. But because I was in denial so deeply—I mean, you could have asked me for a month and I would have never admitted that a particular bruise was from a fist and not a door—they didn't go beyond their initial observation for a long time. My parents knew what was going on, but, like my friends, had no idea how to get me to admit to it, or what to do about it.

—Amy Woods, teen dating violence survivor

There was nothing we could do to stop it. I think as a parent, next to losing a child, the worst thing I can imagine is seeing your child hurting, or in pain, and, short of locking her up, not being able to do anything to protect her from the abuse she's suffering.

—Claire Woods, Amy's mother

A Mother and Daughter Face Reality

"I Was So Tired of Lying": Amy Woods

On January 27, 2000, seventeen-year-old Amy Woods looked in the mirror and hated what she saw. "I was pale, sad, and empty," she recalls. "I couldn't hide it any more." The "it" to which Amy referred was the years of emotional and physical abuse she'd suffered from her boyfriend. (Her story is told in chapters 1 and 2.) She had worked overtime to hide the outward bruises he'd inflicted upon her.

"I never told a soul," Amy says. "Whenever I had bruises, my friends would question me. A couple of times I had a black eye and, when they asked me what happened, I made up excuses: 'I slammed my head in the car door.' Or 'I tripped and hit my head on the doorknob.' My friends would respond, 'Whatever. We know what's really going on.' They always told me they didn't believe the reasons I gave them. But, not knowing what to do, they didn't push matters, either."

Still, as she stared at herself in the mirror on January 27, 2000, Amy knew that, because of what had transpired just moments before, her secret torture-chamber existence had to end. "It was Super Bowl Sunday," she recalls. "I had come home from work at 4 P.M. My boyfriend was supposed to meet me there so that we could spend time together before going over to my grandma's house to be with my family. But 6 P.M. rolled around, and he still wasn't there and hadn't phoned. I was so used to this structure he had set that required us to be together all the time."

When her boyfriend finally arrived, Amy was enraged. "I started to cry and asked him where he'd been," she says. "He had cheated on me often in the past, so I knew that was a possibility. We argued for a little while, and then suddenly, he just exploded. He punched me in my face; he picked up a pillow, put it over my face and started to punch me through it. He'd done that before because he knew hitting me through a pillow wouldn't leave marks. He threw me on the ground and began kicking and stepping on me. He picked up one of my mother's kitchen chairs and tried to slam it over my head. Fortunately, the wooden bar in the middle of the chair prevented this. At one point, I got up and he punched me again, full force, in the middle of my face. I fell back, screaming hysterically."

Amy recalls her boyfriend looking down at her and then running away. Dazed, the seventeen-year-old battered teen slowly got to her feet and realized she was talking to herself. 'I don't understand. I don't understand,' Amy heard herself repeating. She then made her way over to a nearby mirror.

"I started to check, as usual, to see what marks I had to hide," she says. "And I had this huge welt right in the middle of my forehead. I didn't have bangs or long hair, so I knew I wasn't going to be able to hide that bruise. As I continued to look in the mirror I remember, for once, really seeing myself—that is, seeing who I had become. I was so tired of lying. So I called my best friend, I called my sister, I called my mother, and then I called the police."

"Thank God It's Finally Happened": Claire Woods

Claire Woods vividly recalls that fateful Super Bowl Sunday a few years ago. "We were all up at my parent's house watching the game when Amy called. 'Come home. He hit me. I've called the police.' These are the phrases I remember my daughter saying through her tears. And all I could think to myself was 'Thank God, it's finally happened.' I was saddened that Amy had suffered a beating, but I was glad she was finally admitting to the reality of her abusive situation. I didn't want her hurt anymore."

Claire and her husband drove home immediately. Paramedics and police officers were already at the scene. "Amy had a huge knot in the middle of her forehead," Claire recalls. "She shared some of the details about the horrific attack her boyfriend had perpetrated against her."

Still, the enormity of the living hell Amy had experienced during the years she'd dated a violent teenage young man was not impressed upon Claire until the next day. "We went to court that Monday morning to obtain a temporary restraining order (TRO) against Amy's boyfriend," Claire says. "It was an emotionally draining day. Amy had to write out everything he'd ever done to her, which was very traumatizing."

On that long and stressful day in court, Claire first learned the depth and duration of her daughter's torture. Amy's boyfriend had repeatedly punched her in various parts of her body: head, face, mouth, ears, stomach; had burned her with his cigarettes; had dragged her across asphalt; had smashed cell phones over her head; and, Claire learned, he had whipped Amy across her back and arms with a straightened-out metal coat hanger. "I was shocked and saddened over all the abuse my daughter suffered and held deep inside herself for so long," Claire laments.

Even after being granted a TRO, Amy was secretly seeing her abuser. Claire took action. "Intimate partner abuse is such a vicious cycle," Amy's mother says. "When we found out they were seeing each other, we had Amy's boyfriend arrested for violating the TRO. He spent ninety days in jail. The three-month separation allowed Amy time to gain a better perspective. She had a victim witness counselor who was really good. But, as the time for her boyfriend's release from jail neared, my family and I felt scared."

When the young man got out of jail, he stalked Amy. "There were some phone calls and stuff, so we had him rearrested," Claire says. "He was furious at us, but that didn't matter. My job then was to protect my child. So the message my husband and I communicated to Amy was 'You're not able right now to protect yourself. And, as your parents, that's our job.'"

How can spiritual leaders and parents better serve victim-survivors like Amy Woods, while holding to account teens, like her former boyfriend, who perpetrate the crime and sin of intimate partner violence? What are the do's and don'ts that clergy, youth ministers, Christian educators, and parents must consider in their response to both abused and abusive teens? How can church leaders and Christian laity help young Christian women and men to fully accept and embrace gender equality, which is the quintessential message of God, Jesus Christ, and Christian scripture? We'll focus attention on these vital concerns in the rest of this chapter.

Shifts in Thinking

In order for clergy, youth ministers and youth workers, Christian educators and parents to better serve victims-survivors of teen-dating violence as well as hold accountable those teens who perpetrate this crime and sin, there needs to be major shifts in the ways most of us have been raised to think culturally, socially, and theologically. Let's take a close look at three essential shifts: from denial to belief and active response, from barrier building to bridge building, from male domination to gender equality.

Violence Does Occur Here: A Shift from Denial to Belief and Active Response

> Parents and pastors need to know the who, what, why, where, when, and how; that is, the basic facts about dating violence among teens. I think a lot of adults, as well as teens, do not know the broad scope of the problem. For example, most people are not aware of the fact that one in three teens is abused by a boyfriend or girlfriend. That's 33.3 percent of teenagers nationwide. The statistic alone should alert us that dating violence is occurring within our own churches, communities, and homes.
>
> —Gina Graham Palmer, family violence prevention specialist, Alternatives to Domestic Violence, Corona, Calif.

It is essential in any teen dating violence intervention strategy to believe that the problem exists in our churches, communities, and our homes, and then to take appropriate action. When we assume it isn't happening in our families or communities, we leave victimized teens isolated and vulnerable to further torture from their abusive partners. It also means we leave perpetrators of teen dating violence unchecked.

Claire Woods speaks to this issue from personal experience. "Love can be pretty blinding," the mother of Amy says. "The young man who abused my daughter had obviously struck a place in my heart. So it was really difficult for me to see—or want to see—all the abuse he was committing. Thus, one suggestion I have for parents is to make sure they talk with other people, whether at church, at home, or on a hotline, to get a reality check. I was in so much denial about Amy's situation. My husband provided a reality check, which helped me to see matters more clearly."

Denial that teen dating violence happens among Christian youth is a major problem among some spiritual leaders and Christian laity. As was mentioned in chapter 1, the invitations I receive from pastors, lay leaders, and teachers at Christian congregations and high schools to speak on teen dating violence awareness are often accompanied by the request that I "tone down" my language during my presentations. And yet, time and again, the youth attending these sessions have demonstrated that they are not only aware of the negative words, but many of them also disclose that they themselves use the words on a regular basis.

This denial was also apparent as I was conducting research for this volume. More than thirty Christian youth ministers throughout the United States, both females and males, were asked to participate in the project by agreeing to be interviewed. Only three of these spiritual leaders appear in various chapters of this book. Seven other youth pastors admitted that dating violence awareness is not something they address—though all of these female and male leaders said they needed to start dealing with this issue because it is a concern among the youth they serve.

Most significant, however, is the fact that more than twenty Christian youth ministers declined the invitation to be interviewed for this book. Below are the reasons they gave for not participating.

- Dating violence is not a problem among our youth.
- Ours is a white suburban congregation, and teen dating violence occurs most often in black urban areas and on American Indian reservations.
- I'm not ready to open that can of worms.
- We're a conservative congregation; having my name associated with a liberal author and publisher could cost me my position.
- No youth has ever told me they were having a problem with dating violence. (More than five hundred youth attend this youth leader's parish.)
- We're focusing on other social justice issues. (When asked to name one such issue, this particular minister said he didn't have time for my "mean-spiritedness.")
- Our youth are too smart to involve themselves in situations of dating violence.
- We don't believe in premarital sexual activity. (Asked to explain this comment in light of my wanting to conduct an interview on teen dating violence awareness, this particular youth pastor ended our conversation.)

Denial by parents and Christian leaders can leave teen dating violence survivors spiritually scarred. Read the thoughts of Sarah (whose story of abuse at the hands of her Christian boyfriend Lawrence is told in chapters 1 and 2).

I often struggle with the idea of church. I often fight against the messages my denomination and Lawrence perpetuated in my heart and head. I often struggle with the disappointment and anger that I feel toward the church, toward the pastors, and toward people in ministry positions (men and women) who never believed me, never validated me, and never helped me. Because of that, I do not attend church services often. My faith process has not been received well by many Christians that I grew up with or many of the Christians I still know in the denomination I was raised in. Somewhere in the process, I realized that I did not fit in the Christian system anymore. What was once a meaningful and constant part of my life took on meanings of judgment, entrapment, fear, and coercion.

Acknowledging that teen dating violence is a harsh reality in our own churches and communities is essential, but it is not enough. Christian leaders and parents must also be willing to take an active role to help bring an end to abusive situations. Specific guidelines for intervention will be discussed later in this chapter. And, in chapter 5, we'll describe why it is imperative for us to draw on the expertise of a team of lay and professional caregivers when we engage in this work. But one action must be taken immediately: We must always place as our top priority the safety of the victimized teen and her or his family.

In far too many instances, parents, spiritual leaders, and other individuals have compromised a victim-survivor's safety by making their number-one priority the protection of the offender's reputation and future career, or the offender's family's standing in the community. (This is especially the case when the accused is a male.) Many have jeopardized a battered teen's safety when they blame the victim-survivor for her or his own victimization. (This often happens in the case of an abused female.) At other times, well-intentioned parents and Christian leaders who attempt to "rescue" or "save" an abusive teen compromise the victim-survivor's safety.

Claire Woods now realizes some of her responses to Amy's boyfriend's verbal and emotional abuse tactics placed Amy at risk for greater harm. "Even with all [of his emotional abuse] we continued to allow this young man into our house," Claire says. "We became an emergency shelter of some kind. We'd pray together and think, 'Maybe he just needs to see a role model and have a family that supports him.' We didn't understand abuse dynamics at that time. We just wanted to help this young man out."

Nowadays, with the benefit of insight and time, Claire has a different outlook. "As parents, we need to remember that the safety of our children has to be top priority," she says. "The concern is keeping them alive. I was so grateful when that young man really beat Amy up, though I hated the thought of her being hurt. The reason I was so relieved is because this horrific act forced Amy to tell us exactly what was going on. Prior to this incident, she had camouflaged everything. Once all the abuse was out in the open, my husband and I could work on keeping our daughter safe from further harm."

Christian pastors, educators, youth ministers, and youth workers need also to make sure their number-one priority, as they intervene in situations of teen dating violence, is the safety of victimized young adults. I'm especially concerned for situations in which the abused teen is female and her abuser is male. I've observed that many male clergy, ministers, and laity offer excuses for male offenders and blame female victims-survivors for the violence they suffer. (This is vividly illustrated in chapter 3 with the story of the accused teenage son of a Christian pastor. Recall that even though the young man confessed to physically and sexually assaulting his teenage girlfriend, twenty male Christian pastors, including the perpetrating teen's father, vowed to "take a stand"—that is, protect the young man from accountability for his crimes and sins.)

If male clergy, Christian educators, youth ministers, and youth workers continue to assume a misogynic and patriarchal outlook, female Christian teens who are violated by their male Christian partners will remain endangered. And the offending men and boys will have a sense of empowerment and justification. We'll talk further about misogyny and patriarchy and their impact on teen dating violence later in this chapter.

"I Forbid You": A Shift from Barrier-Building to Bridge-Building

> We need to understand that as parents, we have power and control over our children. But over the years, our role has to be one of diminishing power and control.
> —Leah Aldridge, associate director for youth violence prevention, policy, and training, Los Angeles Commission on Assault Against Women

In this section, we'll consider the wisdom of four leaders in the field of teen dating violence prevention and intervention. I asked these "bridge builders" to discuss strategies to help keep youth open to discussing dating issues with parents, pastors, and other adults.

Pick your battles:
Leah Aldridge, youth violence prevention trainer
Leah Aldridge finds herself challenged by her own parental instructions. "My daughter is thirteen; she'll soon be fourteen," she says. "All her life I've told her, 'If you have anything you want to discuss, you can talk to me.' Now she's testing this." What the young teen is seeking to obtain from her mother is

permission to begin wearing gothic-style clothing. "I can't stand that look," Ms. Aldridge says. "I think it's depressing, I think it's overly emotive and overly dramatic, and I don't want my child dressing that way or being perceived that way because we know that when kids dress a particular way they get treated that way. Still, as we were riding in the car the other day, my daughter says 'Mom, I don't want you to get mad but, you know, I kind of like the way the Goth kids dress. So I want to dress that way.'"

Ms. Aldridge says she takes extra caution to not overdramatize her disdain for the gothic style of dress. She also is careful not to risk the chance of tarnishing the open communication she shares with her daughter. "I have to weigh if this is a battle that I really need to fight with my kid," says Ms. Aldridge. "I keep asking myself, 'Is this one of those issues I really want to go to the mat on?' I have to say no. I remind myself that my daughter is not out in the community dressed half-naked, she gets good grades, and, at least not yet, she doesn't present me with a whole lot of issues or troubles."

Recognizing the importance of looking for win-win solutions, the mother poses a compromise to her daughter. "She knows I don't like [the Goth] look," Ms. Aldridge says. "But, I try very hard not to roll my eyes, try not to slam my hand on the dashboard of the car as I'm talking to her, and I try not to wave my hands. Yet, she knows I'm annoyed. Finally, I tell my kid, 'Okay, we'll strike a deal. You don't get to dress that way every day. And, ultimately, since I have to buy the clothes, I get final approval on what is worn.'"

Ms. Aldridge says, as parents, we have been given a great ability to impact the behavior of our children. However our job can be measured in how well our children actualize their authority to impact their own behavior. "Our perceived 'power and control' over our children diminishes with time," she says, "hopefully creating healthy, productive members of society who behave responsibly when mom and dad are not watching."

Remain Open: Daryl Bonilla, educator

Daryl Bonilla cautions parents and Christian leaders to monitor their approach so as not to create barriers with young adults. "Teenagers are weird," he says, "in the sense they're sensitive to the fact that if you initially make a wrong move, they'll close off. So when I'm conducting teen dating violence awareness sessions with the kids, I try to make these times talk story. [A phrase used in Hawaii to describe an informal conversation.] I remain open to whatever teens need to share. In that way, the kids don't feel as though I'm judging them. They are free to express themselves."

Try to listen and understand your teen:
Melissa Thielhelm, children and youth ministries director

"They might not show it in the same manner as us adults, but youth have an amazing desire to know God," says Melissa Thielhelm. "So we adults shouldn't look down on them when they do things differently than us. They want to be fed; they're searching for answers."

Ms. Thielhelm cautions parents not to judge their kids. Instead, she says, parents need to try to communicate with and understand what their children are facing. "I know many parents who'll walk by the tube when MTV is on, roll their eyes, and storm out of the room," she says. "This gives children the message that the parents do not love them enough to talk about what it is about a particular program that they don't like or respect. Or it sends the message that we parents disapprove of the behaviors kids are involved in. This may compel kids to do even more of these behaviors because they realize it makes their parents angry."

Ms. Thielhelm offers an alternative approach to parents. "We need to sit down and watch a little of the program with our children," she says. "Perhaps then, there may be a particular topic that comes up which parents and teens can discuss together. The same can occur if we tune into the radio stations our teens are listening to. Even if what we hear offends us, it may give us the opportunity to share with our teens why we are offended—and to discuss why the music doesn't offend them."

"Empower her": Jill Murray, psychotherapist

"Parents can definitely try to control their daughter out of an abusive relationship by forbidding her from seeing the guy who's violating her," says Dr. Jill Murray. "But that usually doesn't work because it pushes the girl closer to the boy—he's this tragic figure that she needs to save. And it goes to prove that everybody hates him, and she's the only person who will take care of him. So it's actually a kind of boomerang thing. Plus, it reinforces the boy's efforts to isolate the girl from her family. 'Your family doesn't really care about you,' he might say. 'They don't want you to be happy.' It just reinforces his stance."

Dr. Murray suggests that parents work on helping their daughters make their own healthy choices. "What we want to do is empower a girl to make her own decisions," she says. "We really don't want to rag on the boyfriend. Instead, we need to help a girl to start looking at the boy's behavior. For instance, a parent might ask, 'He really doesn't want you to see any of the friends you've had for ten years? Would you call this loving behavior?' Or: 'He calls you at two, three, four o'clock in the morning, so you're unable to sleep. Would you call this loving behavior?' Or: 'You feel like you love him and you believe he loves you? But let's just look at some of his behaviors. Is this the type of behavior that you want in your life?' Or: 'If you yourself had a daughter and she brought home a boyfriend that was just like yours, would you describe the behavior that he's doing to your daughter as loving behavior?'"

Dr. Murray says the questions start teenage girls thinking about the kind of behaviors they want for their lives.

"Why Doesn't God Love Girls?":
A Shift from Male-Dominant to Gender Equal Values

I'd been asked by the principal of a Christian high school to speak with her students about cultural sensitivity. However, some of the sixty-six girls and boys attending this talk had a different concern. As I was weaving through my standard opening exercise, which involves dividing attendees into smaller subgroups with females and males in each to address the question "What's different and similar about us?" I was interrupted by a teenage female who rushed to the front of the class.

"Why doesn't God love girls?" asked the teen in a very serious tone. "If God is the God of all people," she further quizzed, "then why are there certain church positions that females aren't allowed to hold?"

The cultural sensitivity talk was suddenly replaced by a discussion on gender equality. Most of the students, by a show of hands, welcomed the change. I asked the school's principal what she thought of this shift in topic. She called together the faculty, which consisted of six teachers and the pastor of the church to which the school was connected. A few minutes later, I was invited into their huddle and told by the principal and pastor that I could proceed with the topic change, as long as I promised to be "biblical" in my approach. I readily consented to this stipulation.

Asked by me to expound upon her question about God's love of girls, or the lack thereof, the young woman, who I learned was sixteen years old, said "I just don't get it! At home, my mom and dad tell me I can do anything I want. God will guide me, my parents have said. But when I tell them I think God is leading me to prepare for a future in parish ministry, they smile and say, 'Honey, adulthood is a long time from now. God certainly has something special for you—maybe in Christian education, but not parish ministry. We'll see.'" (Recall the words of longtime Christian youth pastor Niki Christiansen in chapter 2: "Leadership roles that tend to have more spiritual responsibilities are usually offered to men. The main exception to this rule is when the position is in Christian education. This feeds the stereotype that, among church leaders, women can have authority only with children.")

The sixteen-year-old female teen said she received an even more pointed response when she spoke to her youth pastor about the "calling" God had placed on her heart. "He laughed at me," she said with sadness. "Then the pastor told me that one day a guy will come along, I'll fall in love with him, we'll marry and have children, and he'll protect the kids and me from harm while taking care of all our needs."

Enraged, the female teen continued. "I don't need someone to protect or take care of me," she said. "How does the youth pastor even know that I'll get married one day, or would even want to? I just want someone to tell me why I'm not allowed to be who I think God is calling me to be, which is a parish pastor."

I decided to bring the other sixty-five Christian high school students in on this discussion. In eleven subgroups made up of six individuals, females and males, I posed a question. Why would God call males, but not females, into parish ministry? Here's what some of the youth had to say. The gender of each respondent is included in parentheses:

- Girls are too emotional. (male)
- The Bible instructs males to lead and females to follow. (male)
- Girls need guys to protect them. (female)
- It's wrong for females to tell males what to do. (male)
- Guys are physically stronger than girls. (male) (Asked if he thought males were also emotionally and spiritually "stronger" than females, he replied "No, not really.")
- I can think of no reason why females can't hold the same exact positions as males. (male)
- Jesus says women should follow men. (male)

- Jesus loves women and girls as much as he loves men and boys. (female)
- There is no reason why females can't be parish pastors; the church is just prejudiced against females. (female)
- Guys are natural church leaders, girls are better at English, math, and in the home. (male)
- Women serve God best when they serve men. (female)
- God is a man, not a woman. (male)
- Men are better than women at making tough decisions, that's why all the presidents [of the United States] have been males. (male)
- The whole idea of male-only parish pastors is stupid; women can lead just as well as men. (male)

The cultural and religious teachings that influenced the above responses from the fifteen and sixteen-year-old Christian youth need to be completely overhauled. These types of beliefs, which include the Christian doctrine of an alleged "God-given" male authority and "God-ordained" female subjugation, set females up for failure and males up for feelings of entitlement and abusive behavior. Women and girls are programmed to think of themselves as less than males or "incomplete" without a boyfriend or husband. As Grace Alvaro Caligtan, the program coordinator of the Teen Alert Program of the Domestic Violence Clearinghouse and Legal Hotline located in Honolulu, observes, "I think the overriding message still today for women, young and old, is that we are nothing without a man. Our value is nothing without being partnered." Meanwhile, the same value system created and condoned by Christian churches and mainstream society that subjugates females entitles males to privileges that allow them to do whatever they desire with girls and women—without fear of accountability for their crimes and sins.

In regard to teen dating violence, adolescent girls who have been indoctrinated under the male-dominant system find it very difficult to free themselves from an abusive male intimate partner. Both church and society have told these young women that they are subordinate to young men, even in God's sight. Hence the sixteen-year-old Christian young woman's question, "Why doesn't God love girls?"

Many women who were abused by their male partners during their teenage years live with spiritual and emotional scars the rest of their lives. Note once again the words of one teen dating violence survivor, Sarah.

I live daily with the physical and spiritual consequences of surviving such a relationship. However, no scars run as deep, nor were integrated as deeply into my perception of myself, as the emotional abuse that Lawrence inflicted on me. During our relationship, I was figuratively beaten down constantly and in many different ways. There are certain things that he said to me about my worth and potential that I have never told anyone about, it simply has hurt that much. I especially struggle with his constant mocking and making fun of me for things that were at the very root of my personality and heart, at the very essence of what made me a human, a woman, and an individual. It took a long time for me to even believe that I and my life were worth rebuilding. Sometimes, I will still hear his voice in my head telling me how worthless he thought I was and how inadequate every one of my efforts would be. During and right after this relationship, I used anything that I could get my hands on to take away the pain. I was abusing medication, legal and illegal. I am very fortunate that drugs did not steal away the rest of whatever life I had. I had to re-learn how to cope with stress, fear, and pain. I had to completely re-learn how to properly care for myself.

Teaching gender equality rather than male dominance to our daughters and sons, while certainly not a cure-all, will surely lessen incidents of male violence perpetrated against females. Women and girls will be more empowered to not accept such inappropriate treatment, while men and boys will feel less entitled, which in turn, will help males accept females as equals rather than subordinates.

Let's return to the high school student's question, "Why doesn't God love girls?" Toward the end of our hour-long discussion on gender equality, the sixty-six Christian female and male youth wanted to know my own personal views on women in ordained ministry. Remembering I had been asked by the principal of the school and pastor of the church located on the same grounds to be "biblical" in my approach, I said "There's nothing in Christian scripture, or in the teachings of God or Jesus Christ, to support keeping women out of any aspect of ministry. Practices that support a male-dominant and female subordinate position run contrary to the overarching views of God and Jesus Christ. We are all one in Christ Jesus. It makes no sense that a God of compassion, equality, love, and mercy, and a Christ of mutuality and justice, would order women and men in a hierarchy."

In unison, the young women and men rose to their feet and applauded. They asked if I would consider returning to the school in the future for further discussions on this topic. If I was invited by the principal, faculty, and pastor to return, I would do so gladly, I said.

Following class, the principal asked me to join her and the pastor in her office. "You led us to believe, Rev. Miles, that you would be biblical in addressing this topic," she chided. "All you did was spit on the beliefs of this fine institution, give girls false information about their role in church and society, and tear down the leadership position that boys must assume. You've done a grave disservice." The pastor said nothing, but his nods gave approval to the principal's tongue-lashing.

There has been no follow-up invitation for me to speak at this particular Christian high school.

Ending Violence: Guidelines for Parents and Pastors

In the final section of this chapter we'll offer specific guidelines for parents and parish leaders (clergy, Christian educators, youth ministers, and youth workers) on teen dating violence intervention strategies. Though parents have different roles, authority, and responsibility over youths' lives than parish leaders do, they have similar principles to follow. However, there are some guidelines specific to each group. I offer comments throughout the section from experts in the field of dating violence awareness, from survivors, and from the teens themselves.

Guidelines for Parents

Recognize the reality of dating violence.

There are teens living in our communities and worshiping in our churches who are in violent relationships. Some of our own daughters and sons are in violent relationships. (Refer to chapter 1 for a review of specific warning signs.)

Make the safety of a victimized teen top priority.

Remember the words of Claire Woods, mother of a teen dating abuse survivor: "The concern is keeping [our children] alive." While it is appropriate to also worry about the well-being of an abusive teen and to pray for him, parents must not let this overshadow their concern for the safety of the victim-survivor. Also, we must avoid being the "rescuer" or "savior" of an abusive teen. Perpetrators are often very manipulative and slick. They will misuse our compassion, and even our Christian traditions and values, to trick us into believing their abusive behavior has ceased. Most often, this is not the case without long-term, offender-specific, professional treatment.

Listen to and talk with your children.

This needs to begin very early in a child's life and continue throughout adulthood. "If we don't have an open and honest relationship with our teens to begin with, then they're going to be reluctant to share important and pertinent information about things such as episodes of dating violence," cautions Lisa Brito Greene, the mother of eighteen-year-old son, Akijuwon. "Parents must also not shut teens down; we need to learn to listen. As adults, we have the tendency to talk, and our listening takes a backseat. If we're totally incapable of hearing what our teens have to say, then we need to direct them to other adults who will listen to them."

The different people interviewed for this volume repeated the importance of listening to and talking with teens. If parents are willing to hear what their daughters and sons are saying, even if there are disagreements, it is more likely that these young women and men will share with their parents important information about their lives. Consider the words of two teenagers. "Parents must listen, without being judgmental, to what their kids are telling them," says nineteen-year-old Chris Stumpff of Cedar Rapids, Iowa, and a member of Ta Da, Teens Against Domestic Abuse and Violence. Chris believes that parents can establish trust if they will listen and talk with their teenage children without overreacting to what the youth have to say. "Parents need to build a trust foundation with their kids," he says. "In that way, if a kid is in an abusive relationship, she or he will be much more likely to let the parent know exactly what is going on."

Seventeen-year-old Vanessa Silver of Norco, California, agrees. "Parents need to talk to their kids and get involved in their lives," she says. "But teens must be talked to as young adults instead of as young children."

Have candid and open discussions with teens about human sexuality.
Parents need to talk about their beliefs, expectations, and values about human sexuality—but without making statements that seem judgmental or appear to be ultimatums. Discussing sexuality with teens is a major hurdle for some parents, especially those who are Christians. There is a pervasive belief that if we speak frankly with our daughters and sons about their sexuality (except for when we promote sexual abstinence and sexual purity) then we are encouraging our children to engage in sexual activity. Because my presentations, books, and articles include candid discussion of sexual intercourse and outercourse, anal sex, oral sex, mutual masturbation, sexual abuse and sexual assault, sexually transmitted diseases, and about what is actually involved in making sex consensual, many Christian parents and pastors have accused me of encouraging teens to engage in sexual activities.

In reality, most adolescents, Christians and non-Christians alike, are already involved in sexual activities. And if parents refuse to discuss human sexuality with them, these young adults are forced to learn about this essential topic from their peers or popular culture, especially various media.

"Just because we go to church doesn't mean we're not experiencing the same problems other teens face, such as drugs, sex, and violence," says Vanessa Silver. "For example, if a teen is dating or feeling close to someone, then parents need to come straight out and ask their son or daughter if they're having or thinking about having sex. Even though the parents can't really stop them from engaging in sexual activity—I mean, if they're going to do it, they're going to do it—parents can tell their teens about consequences resulting from their choices, like contracting STDs or becoming pregnant."

Vanessa reminds parents to talk with—rather than at—their children. "If parents say 'I forbid you to have sex,' that won't be helpful at all," she insists. "Teens need to feel appreciated and respected."

Shari Miller, the program coordinator for the Youth Leadership Program of the Community Corrections Improvement Association in Cedar Rapids, Iowa, speaks on the topic of teen sexuality as both a Christian and the mother of an eighteen-year-old son. "Sexuality is an essential part of our nature," she says. "I think the problem is so many people deny this fact." Ms. Miller believes it's vital for parents to talk candidly with their teenage children about the broader aspects of sexuality. "It's been narrowed into just a physical act, rather than one of the greatest gifts we humans have been given by God," she says. "If we can explain sexuality in the latter way to our children, and also articulate the great deal of responsibility which comes with this gift, that would be wonderful."

Maintain open lines of communication.
Parents must not judge harshly the behavior or choices their teenage children make. The goal is to stay connected. "Because I was angry and frustrated over what I perceived as Amy's not standing up for herself," says Claire Woods, "I'd say things like 'I taught you better than this.' Or 'We raised you better than that.'" The mother now admits this particular approach was not helpful. "I now realize that these types of phrases might infer to a victim that she's a failure." Her daughter responded more positively, Claire says, when concerns were expressed less confrontationally. "I tried to avoid deep and stressful conversations with Amy," Claire explains. "I know my daughter. She's the type of person who doesn't like to be backed into a corner."

Making judgmental comments about an abusive teen partner or relationship is risky. Usually, this forces the victim-survivor into a no-win situation. Dr. Jill Murray offers an example of the dangers involved in such an approach. "If you judge the relationship of your teen daughter," she says, "even if you know that it's unhealthy and that the guy is a creep and that she doesn't deserve this type of treatment, it'll just push her farther away from you and make her feel like she can never talk to you again. Remember, she's been brainwashed by the guy. She's really like a concentration camp survivor. So trying to stay connected with her is really important."

Stay apprised of teen activities and relationships.
"Children need parents," says Melissa Thielhelm, children's and youth ministries director at Hope Reformed Church in Sheboygan, Wisconsin. "There are so many parents who want to be their child's best friend. Children want someone who will set limits with them, someone who will say 'No, you can't stay out until midnight,' 'No, your boyfriend can't sleep over.' I think the setting of limits makes kids feel loved."

In addition, be aware of the articles and books your daughters and sons read, the movies and videos they watch, the music they listen to, the sites they visit on the Internet, and the company they keep. You have the responsibility to monitor the activities of your daughters and sons, and if you discover something that causes you concern, express your feelings and thoughts to the teens directly. Bear in mind that offering judgmental statements or ultimatums rarely help these situations. In fact, doing so runs the great risk of discouraging honest sharing from teens.

Teens themselves speak to the importance of parental involvement. "Parents need to pay close attention to the age group of the people their children are around," says Jordon Goettsche. "If a younger teen girl, for example, is hanging out with older guys, then there's probably going to be situations when she begins to date one of them. Those are the circumstances where I've seen guys take advantage of these young and naïve girls." Vanessa Silver adds, "Parents need to also find out more about all the activities we're involved in."

Recognize the far-reaching impact of abuse.

Be aware of the fact that if your daughter or son is being abused by a dating partner, she or he is most likely dealing with several other issues as well. These might include depression, decreased academic performance, isolation, lowered self-esteem, engaging in risky sexual activity, substance abuse, and an overall sense of loss of one's self. "As a result of Lawrence's constant sexual disregard for my body," says teen dating violence survivor Sarah, "I remain susceptible to a variety of infections and have even had surgery to correct the internal damage caused by him. And yet the physical consequences I consider almost minimal when compared to the damage Lawrence's abuse did to me emotionally."

Focus on what's most important.

Because abuse has a wide range of effects as described above, parents need to choose carefully the issues they will address with firmness (remember to avoid judgmental statements or giving ultimatums) and those that have room for compromise. For example, while parents may not like the type of clothing their teen daughter is wearing or her tattoos, they should weigh these concerns against her receiving fifty phone calls a day from her boyfriend, her fear of him, and the unexplained bruises popping up all over her body. In other words, parents must be careful not to alienate their abused teen over clothing choice or tattoos. If the connection is lost between parents and teens, it is far less likely that teens will confide in parents when they are experiencing violence from a dating partner.

Seek support for yourself.

In the midst of caring for daughters and sons affected by dating violence, it is important for parents to seek support for themselves. Counselors, family members, friends, clergy, Christian educators, youth ministers, and youth workers can provide guidance, a listening ear, and prayer in the midst of overwhelming situations.

Guidelines for Pastors
Recognize the reality of dating violence.
Parish leaders need to acknowledge that there are teens worshiping in our churches who are in violent relationships. "I think it's critical for pastors to realize that dating violence is a problem that can affect even the most faithful church attending family," says Rick Roberts, pastor of Children and Family Ministries at Kenosha Bible Church in Kenosha, Wisconsin.

Pastor Rick believes that conversations with Christian youth on dating violence must be candid. "It's something that young people, from preadolescence all the way through the teenage years and even into college, need to have frank discussions about," he says. "Parents, as well as youth pastors, youth workers, and Sunday School teachers, should also attend these discussions. The goal is to make sure that the kids and adults have a clear understanding of what a negative relationship looks like," says Pastor Rick, "so that the kids can have a better chance to avoid these types of relationships."

Make the safety of a victimized teen top priority.
Pastors and other parish workers need to be careful not to compromise a victimized Christian teen's safety by what they do or say. For example, when the abusive person is male and the individual abused is female, many male parish leaders may offer excuses for the offender and blame the victim-survivor. Leaders may also hesitate to confront a teen male abuser for fear of "ruining" his chances of a future career. Actually, the best way to "save" the perpetrating male's future career and help him to become a healthy member of church and society is to hold him accountable for his crimes and sins. This will also help to better ensure healing and safety for the teenage female he victimized.

In addition, pastors and other Christian leaders must be willing to partner with service providers in their community. Pastors have a vital role in caring for victimized teens and holding abusers accountable. But pastors and church leaders must know their limits. More about these partnerships will be discussed in chapter 5.

Seek education and training.
Christian leaders can be a tremendous resource to victimized teens, those who perpetrate abuse, and to the parents of both. But we must first receive the appropriate education and training. Otherwise, our well-intentioned efforts can cause more harm than good. "It scares me to think about the number of pastors who say they want to 'get on board' with this issue," says Niki Christiansen, the youth pastor at West Court Street Church of God in Flint, Michigan. "The fear I have is that these pastors will go headlong into something [like teen dating violence awareness] with a real lack of knowledge or understanding of what needs to happen. And they could end up making things worse instead of better."

Teach the equal value of females and males.
Abuse and violence in teen and adult Christian relationships is often encouraged by the male hierarchical teachings and traditions taught by clergy, Christian educators, and youth pastors. Although these constructs do not cause teen dating violence or adult intimate partner abuse, some males use them as rationalizations for whatever they choose to do to females. In turn, these constructs cause women young and old to internalize their alleged "God-ordained" subservient role in both church and society. Male Christian leaders need to take the lead in teaching equal value to females and males.

For example, the concept of male headship and female submission sets up an imbalance of power in a marriage or other intimate partnerships, making it much easier for men to abuse women (and teen boys to abuse teen girls), and then claim divine privilege. Also, Christian men (and boys) need to familiarize themselves with inclusive-language versions of the Bible. The more we espouse egalitarian constructs, the better chance we have truly to live out the ideal of equality and mutuality between women and men (and girls and boys).[1]

Open the door.
If clergy, Christian educators, youth pastors, and youth workers preach and teach on teen dating violence awareness, then more youth will discuss the problem with them. It is imperative before broaching the topic in classrooms, sermons, and at youth gatherings, for parish leaders to first receive the proper education and training in dating violence awareness. "I think when a church doesn't open the door [to allow youth to talk about dating violence] then abuse among teen dating partners in the congregation stays silent," Niki Christiansen says. "As spiritual leaders, we have, unfortunately, tended to deny and avoid this issue altogether. And many of us don't think it's a door that needs to be opened at all."

If we Christian leaders do not discuss emphatically the violence occurring in teen dating relationships in our midst, then who will help our daughters and sons? We must open the door so that young people will have a better chance to live out their adult lives free from the abuse and violence that is destroying so many.

Conclusion
Parents and pastors: Who do we want to provide guidance and support to teens? If an adolescent has questions about sexuality, gender equality, or teen dating violence, do we want them to gain their knowledge on these critical subjects from

their peers or, worse yet, from the media? Are we prepared to engage in an open dialogue with youth about their choice of dating partners, friends, movies, music videos, and Internet sites? Will we remain open to them even if what they listen to or view or share with us is, in our opinion, objectionable? Or will we judge them harshly and offer ultimatums?

Parents and pastors have a major role in helping to ensure the safety and well-being of Christian youth experiencing abuse from a dating partner. When we accept that the crime exists, even among teens who attend worship and youth gatherings on a regular basis, we take an important step in the right direction. When we place the safety of violated teens as our top priority, listen to and believe their horrific stories, provide open and nonjudgmental pathways for dialogue, and treat youth, in the words of seventeen-year-old Vanessa Silver, as young adults instead of as young children, then there's even greater hope that abused teens will be able to break free from the violence that has them incarcerated.

Parents and pastors: Who do we want to provide guidance and support to our teens? The true answer lies with the approach we choose to take with these young women and men.

Questions for Discussion

1. How did you feel as you read about the severe beating Amy Woods suffered from her boyfriend? What steps would you yourself take to help her get to safety? Elaborate.

2. Are teens experiencing dating violence in your church? If yes, what are Christian leaders and laity doing to address this problem? If no, tell why you think the problem of dating violence has not occurred in your midst.

3. As a senior pastor, youth minister, or Christian educator, have you preached or taught on the subject of teen dating violence awareness? If yes, what approach did you take? If no, tell why you have not addressed this topic.

4. How do you feel, as a parent or pastor, about talking with youth about human sexuality? What concerns do you have about broaching this topic?

5. Does your church believe that females can be senior and associate pastors? If not, what is the biblical basis for this exclusion? If so, what biblical and spiritual base is there?

6. As a result of reading this chapter, what will you do differently as a parent or pastor about addressing the subject of teen dating violence? Be specific.

5.

Healthy Teen Dating Relationships: Why Teamwork Is Essential

I always emphasize strengths. I try to get the teens thinking from a positive perspective and hope that, as they practice talking positively about themselves, it will become habit.

—Kelly Ritzman, staff counselor, Rape and Domestic Abuse Center, Sioux Falls, South Dakota

In the previous four chapters we focused on the causes and effects of dating violence among teens who are victimized and those who perpetrate this crime and sin. We learned that Christian teens are in no way shielded from this pervasive problem. In fact, in certain situations, they may even be more vulnerable than non-Christians. For instance, a Christian teen that has been sexually assaulted by a dating partner might be reluctant to disclose this information to her or his parents or pastor, fearing that the adults will judge them as having consensual sex, rather than seeing them as a victim of a crime. And some Christian parents and pastors tend to deny the reality that emotional, physical, and spiritual abuse is occurring within the dating relationships of churchgoing teens. The false belief that a follower of Jesus Christ would never engage in abusive behaviors is widespread. Some parents and pastors profess a theology that places females in subservient positions to males—even to those males who perpetrate violence. As a result, violated Christian teens often feel isolated and trapped in relationships that many of them describe as a type of hell on earth.

Chapters 1 through 4 also revealed the strong influence that popular culture, especially the media, has on Christian and non-Christian youth. Teens' thoughts and feelings about crucial issues such as body image, dating practices, self-esteem, and sexuality have been influenced by what they hear and view in popular music recordings and videos, television, and movies. A recent survey, for example, suggests that watching sex on television predicts and may hasten adolescent sexual initiation. [1]

Concerning the matter of human sexuality, Christian teens also face special struggles. Having received the message from their parents and pastors that sexual intercourse prior to marriage is strictly forbidden (an edict given far more stridently to girls than boys), many churchgoing teens instead engage in sexual activities like anal sex, oral sex, sexual outercourse, and mutual masturbation, thinking that these do not compromise their virginity. These activities place teens at great risk for sexually transmitted diseases and unwanted pregnancies. They also cause many youth to experience spiritual turmoil and feelings of being used, especially after the dating relationship ends. Some teens even report losing a sense of true intimacy. As Dr. Jill Murray stated in chapter 2, "For many teens, sex isn't anything sacred, anything intimate, anything personal, or anything involving a loving interaction; sex is just bodies having sex."

What are the qualities of a healthy teen dating relationship? Are there curricula, homilies, programs, and videos to help parents and pastors offer teens guidance? Why is it essential for all of us to work together as a team if teens are to establish and maintain healthy dating relationships? These questions are the focus of this chapter. To begin, let's check in on the spiritual and emotional lives of the three survivors of teen dating violence who have courageously and unselfishly shared their stories throughout this book. These women chose to participate so that parents and pastors might learn how to better help youth in dangerous and unhealthy relationships.

Survivors Who Are in the Process of Healing

"It has taken me a long time": Sarah

> Intimate relationships, specifically, have been difficult for me since Lawrence's and my relationship. However, [his abuse] has [also] affected every single one of my close friendships. I never really know if I can fully trust anyone, especially the people who tell me that they love me. In dating relationships, I don't think that I ever feel safe enough to be emotionally vulnerable, to express my doubts and fears, and to even express feelings of love. It scares me that at some point the person could choose to use [my expression of love] to hurt me. It has taken me a long time to take the risk of being in another dating relationship. Having been through this [abusive] experience, I have needed the qualities of honesty, kindness, genuineness, consistency, respect, and patience in both an intimate relationship and in friendships.
>
> In the process of regaining my life, I have put such a different value and appreciation on who it is that I am and who people are, the qualities of character that I am developing and the activities and people who I have chosen to

be a part of my life. It took every ounce of my effort to attempt to get [my life] back. And although nothing was good about [my relationship with Lawrence] and nothing is good about the consequences that I deal with daily, in the process of healing I've been given the opportunity to create an entirely new life. The process of healing has given me choices and freedom and, because of that, I think that I have learned what it truly means for me to live. And I am daily learning how to walk into purpose and light.

"I still get angry at God over what happened to me": Angie

After being stabbed by my ex-boyfriend, I was really angry at God. I'd say, "If God's so great, if God's so good, then why would he let something like that happen to good people?" I do consider myself a good person. I still get angry at God over what happened to me, but not as much as I used to. I still don't understand why God allowed this type of violence to happen to me.

Now I'm not so insecure. I can actually walk into a room without crossing my arms and staring down. I walk around looking up and smiling. And I have conversations with anybody, no matter who they are and how they're dressed. I'm just so positive. Still, at times I feel insecure and have a low self-esteem. But neither of these issues is as bad as they used to be because I now surround myself with positive people. And whenever I do this, my self-esteem goes sky high.

"It took me a long time to really have faith in my God": Amy Woods

I was not spiritual during the dating relationship I had with [my ex-boyfriend]. My whole life, my whole soul and being were focused on that relationship. Directly after it ended, I was left with a time of loneliness. As a result, I ended up discovering my spirituality and it really helped me to start to define who I am, who I had been, and who I was not anymore. I always tell people "The person that I was died on January 27, 2000. And the person who I am today is somebody else. That old person doesn't even exist anymore." My spirituality is one of my saving graces.

The one religious thing I remember asking during my relationship with my ex-boyfriend was, "God, where are you? I cry out to you, but you're not here." Afterward, I discovered that my God was always there with me. When I sat crying, God was there. But it took me a long time to really have faith in my God.

Qualities of a Healthy Teen Dating Relationship

Robotic Interlude

In Part III of the three-video series *Love—All That and More* is a vignette titled "Jamal's Blind Date." As the scene opens, we see a man in his late teens, Jamal, speeding toward us in his Jeep. He stops in front of the house of a friend, another teen male, and races to the door. "Man, is she here?" Jamal asks his friend with excitement. "She's so here, so now, so waiting for you," the friend replies. Standing over by a glowing fireplace with her back turned to us is a tall, shapely female teen. When she turns to face Jamal, he is left breathless by her physical beauty. What follows is the brief conversation Jamal has with this young woman and his male friend.

Female: Hi, how're you doing?
Jamal: Say Baby.
Female: I'm Jill, I'm Jill, I'm Jill.
Jamal: What's going on?
Male Friend: She's a robot.

Jamal: A robot? Why am I trying to date a robot instead of a real girl?

Male Friend: Didn't you say you wanted to have a relationship without conflict? Didn't you say you wanted a girl to agree with you at all times about anything? Ain't nobody human like that.

The vignette offers a humorous yet powerful message: Only by having a robot for a partner can a person enjoy a conflict-free dating relationship. It is important not to equate mundane conflict with emotional, physical, sexual, and spiritual abuse. In order for a relationship to be described as healthy, partners must deal with conflict with mutual power and mutual respect. A relationship can never be considered healthy when there are any signs or threats of abuse or violence. Never.

Themes

FaithTrust Institute of Seattle, Washington (www.faith-trustinstitute.org), the producer of *Love—All That and More*, provides a comprehensive curriculum to accompany the video series, plus two discussion facilitators' guides, one for work with Christian youth and the other for work with Jewish youth. The curriculum and facilitators' guides all suggest themes for youth and young adults to watch for to help them determine if their dating relationships are healthy or unhealthy. Among the themes:

- Love alone is not enough for a healthy relationship. Partners need skills for sharing power, resolving conflicts, handling jealousy, building trust, communicating effectively, and knowing how and when to compromise.
- Some degree of jealousy is a natural feeling that comes from insecure feelings about ourselves and our partner's commitment to the relationship. Jealousy becomes

abusive when it is used to dominate and control another person.

- Signs of extreme jealousy include your partner's demanding to know where you are at all times, not wanting you to have your own friends or spend time with other people, and always expecting you to be available to him or her. Extreme jealousy is not a sign of "love;" it is your partner's attempt to control your life. This kind of jealousy is a red flag that could indicate future dating violence.
- When you trust someone, you make yourself vulnerable to being hurt if they let you down.
- Lying to someone, even about little things, teaches them that they cannot trust you.
- Good communication requires talking and listening—really listening. Communication is impaired when one partner doesn't take the other's feelings seriously, bullies or blames the other, or is more concerned about being right than listening with an open heart and mind.
- Good communication is impossible when one partner is afraid of the other.
- Compromise and negotiation are effective strategies for resolving conflict when both people have equal power and respect for each other's rights and values.
- You have the right to end a relationship at any time. You should not be forced to stay in a relationship. While breaking up is never easy, it is often necessary in the search for a healthy relationship.[2]

Balance

Shari Miller, the program coordinator for a youth leadership program in Cedar Rapids, Iowa, works with some teens who are in healthy dating relationships. She talks specifically about one couple. "Their relationship is not out of need," she says. "They are both involved in a multitude of activities outside of their own relationship. So they have a real sense of balance. In other words, while the relationship is important to them, it's not their whole lives."

Staying Connected to Other Friends and Family

Ms. Miller also stresses the important role of friends and family to the health and well-being of a dating couple. "They have mutual friends, and their parents and other family members like each other," she says. "I think these other relationships are important because it prevents one dating partner from isolating the other. I really worry when isolation is a part of any relationship. Our families know us; they have a pretty good sense if someone we're seeing is healthy, supportive, and a good fit, as opposed to having attributes that the family would find unacceptable."

Honesty, Respect, and Care for Each Other

Ms. Miller discussed other qualities of this healthy relationship. The two partners "respect each other, care about each other, and support each other," she said. "But they also seem to clearly understand that it's a high-school dating relationship, and not necessarily a lifelong commitment."

One other point needs to be made here about healthy teen-dating relationships. Youth, parents, and pastors must pay close attention to how and when young people use the phrase "I love you." This is not to suggest that teens cannot feel "true" love; they most certainly can. But abusive teen boys or girls may use the phrase "I love you" to control and dominate their partners and get what they want. "If a guy learns the power (for many girls) of the phrase 'I love you,' then I think he'll say this to get his way in a number of areas, sexually and otherwise," said Melissa Thielhelm, a director of children's and youth ministries at a church in Sheboygan, Wisconsin. "He'll especially do this if he discovers the girl is longing to be loved."

Jordan Goettsche, a nineteen-year-old from Cedar Rapids, Iowa, agrees. "The most confusing part of teenage relationships is love," he said. "Many teens use this word but have no idea what it means. Many males use this word to get sex from girls. Girls think if a guy says 'I love you' that he really means it, and it makes her feel good, even if it is said only a week into the relationship.

"Teenage relationships should not be based on sex and misuse of the word love," Jordan continued. "If every time a guy says 'I love you' to a girl and she has sex with him, he's going to mean it less and less every time he says it. Many teens are in relationships like this, and I think parents need to remember to have talks with their kids about sex and explain healthy relationships."

While these two individuals' observations refer to an abusive male's behavior, young people and pastors should be aware that abusive teen females may also use the phrase "I love you" to manipulate their partners.

Modeling Healthy Dating Relationships

What can parents, clergy, Christian educators, youth, youth ministers, and youth workers do to assist teenage females and males in establishing and maintaining healthy dating relationships? Here are a variety of practices, programs, and resources that advocates, activists, counselors, educators, parents, pastors, and teens themselves use to help adolescents develop good relationships.

Parental Perspectives

A father reflects on raising a daughter:
Rev. Curtiss Paul DeYoung

> When it comes to raising children, especially teenagers
> in the twenty-first century, it often seems like a mystery

to me. Sometimes I really do not know what to do or say. Parenting requires a lot of prayer. I cannot imagine the challenge of single parenting. I am blessed to have the resource of being married to a great parent. I clearly see my parenting as done in the context of a partnership with my wife, Karen.

I believe that the way I value and love Karen has set a high standard for our daughter. Rachel's expectations for how she should be treated in a relationship have been shaped by how I treat her mother. For better or worse, the parents' marriage is a primary influence on a child's understanding of dating relationships. Karen and I have sought to instill in Rachel the perception that she does not need to find a man to be a complete person. I also try to be involved in Rachel's life. I express interest in the issues that engage her and the dreams for the future that inspire her. I affirm her gifts and talents. I also look for opportunities to have fun with her. Sometimes that includes a good laugh about something.

I also invite Rachel into my life. I talk with Rachel about my work and my interests. I ask for her wisdom. I treat her as a person of worth who has valuable viewpoints. This is not a strategy for building positive self-esteem. I really believe that she has much to offer me. As a part of my work I travel. Rachel has joined me on some extended trips. In one case we traveled to South Africa for two weeks. These times have allowed us to form a close bond. She has also been able to observe firsthand my life and work.

I try hard not to be judgmental of Rachel. She is not expected to conform to a predetermined parental expectation for what she should believe. This freedom of thought sometimes leads her in directions that differ from her parents. This is not easy to accept. Yet we respect her right to be her own person. We invite her to express her opinions even when they differ from ours. We certainly offer her guidance and wisdom from having lived life for many more years than she has. We do set boundaries for our children in the area of behavioral choices and respect for the values we hold. Yet the goal that Karen and I seek is to love our children completely and unconditionally.

A mother reflects on raising a son: Shari Miller

Unfortunately, I don't think there is any special recipe or magic formula for raising a happy, healthy teenage son. Wouldn't that be nice? Two cups of love, one cup of discipline . . . but, as we know, it just doesn't work that way. I do know that children are a gift from God and that I've been blessed with the privilege of sharing my life with my beautiful eighteen-year-old son, Nicolas. As much as I'd like to take credit for incredible parenting skills, I know that in reality it is by the grace of God that Nic is the strong, kind young man he is today.

Raising Nic has been an opportunity to learn firsthand about the real meaning of love. Nic has taught me patience, strength, courage, and humility. I've been pushed to my limits and learned that there really is always more to give.

I believe the foundation of my relationship with Nic has been mutual trust. I am the first person he turns to when he is confused and hurting or just needs to talk. He knows that I love him unconditionally and that I will never judge him. I may not like or agree with his actions, but I always make it perfectly clear that no matter what he ever does or says, I love him with all of my heart. And even though I am Nic's parent, I've been willing to show him my own shortcomings and vulnerabilities. I let him see that I am human and that I struggle. He knows that I cry and that sometimes I am afraid. By sharing my ups and downs, I've let Nic know it is okay not to be perfect.

I've found it important to pick my battles with Nic. I've always encouraged him to be an individual and gave him the freedom to be himself as much as possible. I didn't always like his choice in clothes or the way he wore his hair, but I kept my mouth shut and let him express himself. I think that kids who are given no personal freedom tend to act out in bigger ways and an important aspect of the teenage years is defining one's individuality.

In relating to Nic, I've tried to remember what it was like when I was a teenager. Even as a middle-aged mother, I can conjure up memories of the days when life felt like a rollercoaster that didn't end and peer approval seemed paramount. I know that I have to respect Nic's moods and wait until he is ready to talk about things. If I approach him when he isn't ready to share, I might as well be talking to a brick wall and it just causes frustration for both of us.

As a mother, I believe it has been my responsibility to teach Nic to treat women with respect and kindness. I don't believe that men and women are born knowing how to be in relationship with each other. I've tried to keep the lines of communication open so that Nic wouldn't feel silly asking me about girls and romance and how to treat a woman. And I haven't hesitated to give him feedback when I've felt that he has made choices that don't honor women completely. In a culture filled with unhealthy messages about human sexuality and gender equality, I've found it vitally important to counter the negative messages that Nic receives with my own positive message of what a healthy, mutually respectful relationship entails.

Being a parent isn't about having all of the answers; it is about opening your heart and letting God shine through.

Dads and Daughters

Dads and Daughters (DADs) is the national advocacy nonprofit for fathers and daughters. DADs inspires fathers to actively and deeply engage in the lives of their daughters and galvanizes fathers and others to transform the pervasive cultural messages that devalue girls and women.[3]

Daughters: For Parents and Girls is the bimonthly newsletter of Dads and Daughters. It provides parents with information and support intended to help them communicate with and enjoy the company of their adolescent daughters. If communication breaks down or severe problems develop, *Daughters* urges parents to seek the help of professionals.[4] The publication deals with such important issues as communicating, girl athletes and eating disorders, living with a disabled sibling, making good friendship choices, and teaching kids about family finances.

In its March/April 2002 issue, *Daughters* published an article on the dangers of teen-dating violence. The topic was addressed candidly and offered realistic and sound suggestions.

> Even the most empowering upbringing will not absolutely protect her. Believing that "My daughter is too smart for that" may comfort a parent, but it's dangerous for a daughter.[5] You can't control what your girl does away from home. You may have to get school personnel involved. It could be as simple as asking a teacher to bring in a guest speaker on dating violence, so that all the kids get informed and your girl doesn't feel singled out. The bottom line, though, is that you will have to prohibit an abusive relationship if your daughter doesn't do it on her own.[6] (For more information on Dads and Daughters and *Daughters: For Parents and Girls* see Appendix B.)

Peer and Professional Perspectives

Healthy modeling through group counseling: Teen Relationships Group, Rape and Domestic Abuse Center
The Teen Relationship Group is a program of the Rape and Domestic Abuse Center (RDAC) located in Sioux Falls, South Dakota. The group is therapeutic and educational. It offers support for females ages thirteen to seventeen. Goals of this group are:

- To prevent teens from engaging in abusive relationships,
- To help teens to distinguish between healthy and unhealthy dating relationships,
- To help teens who choose to end an unhealthy dating relationship to do so in a manner that will offer them the best possibility of safety,
- To enhance self-esteem.

Group topics include:

- High risk relationships,
- Healthy self-esteem,
- Coping with current or past abuse,
- Nonviolent problem solving,
- Power and control.

The group consists of eight, one-hour sessions occurring on a weekly basis. It is limited to five members.

Kelly Ritzman, a licensed professional counselor in South Dakota who is also certified nationally, has worked for RDAC for the past two-and-a-half years. One of her roles with the agency is to facilitate the Teen Relationships Group.

"I use several techniques in my work with girls to help them develop their own style," Ms. Ritzman says. "I respect each teen for her individuality. I let them know I value their opinions. I don't behave in such a way as to convey that I think I am better than they are because I'm an adult, or for any other reason." Ms. Ritzman says she also encourages teen girls to challenge negative beliefs society holds about females. "We talk about media stereotypes and how they are used," she says. "I let the girls know that the media is concerned with selling products, and not with helping individuals meet their goals for personal growth. Being a physically beautiful and ultra thin female works well for the media because this exploits insecurities of consumers. However, I let group members know that when we admire ourselves for who we are on the inside, we thwart the media's efforts at making our society superficial."

Because society overemphasizes aesthetics in females, Ms. Ritzman says she shies away from complimenting girls on their physical appearance. "I believe doing so sends a strong negative message to females in our society," she says. "I do not want to teach girls that their self-worth is determined by what they look like on the outside. Of course, when a teen is proud of a new outfit or hairstyle I will validate her. But I try to teach these young women to be proud of their inner selves. They can enjoy compliments, I say, but I want to help them to understand that they don't need compliments from other people to feel good about themselves. I would like all teens to realize that self-worth comes from within."

Healthy modeling through creativity: "We Can Wait"
Daryl Bonilla is an educator for the Domestic Violence Clearinghouse and Legal Hotline in Honolulu. Through the agency's Teen Alert Program, Daryl and his colleagues speak to about two hundred youth each month. He has written a number of plays, scenarios, and skits to dramatize for teens the qualities of healthy and unhealthy dating relationships.

"We Can Wait" is one of the skits. "I came up with this concept to help show kids that there is a way to wait to have sex and still have a wonderful time with your dating partner,"

Daryl explains. "We want kids to be respectful to their dating partners, and to themselves, by respecting the other person's wishes. We use another skit I wrote as a companion piece to 'We Can Wait.' In that situation, a male uses techniques such as guilt to coerce his girlfriend into having sex. 'We Can Wait' shows the opposite of this, the positive and respectful way."

"We Can Wait"

(Doug and Janine are both students. They both like each other but have not been serious. They have gone out with their friends as a group. This is their first time being alone. They are sitting on the couch in Doug's home.)

Doug: You want something to drink?

Janine: I'm okay. Thanks. I had a great time at the movies.

Doug: Yeah, me too. The movie wasn't that good, but I liked the other part. You know, the being-with-you part.

Janine: Yeah.

Doug: Yeah. I really like you Janine.

Janine: I like you too, Doug.

(Doug leans in to kiss Janine but she turns her head.)

Doug: What's wrong?

Janine: Nothing. It's just that your parents might come home.

Doug: They won't be back until a couple of hours.

(Doug leans in to kiss her again and once again she turns away.)

Doug: I thought you liked me.

Janine: I do, but I want to take things slow. I want to get to know you better.

Doug: I thought you wanted me to do something. That's why you asked to come over after you heard my parents were out.

Janine: To talk. I wanted to be alone with you and talk.

Doug: So you don't want to do anything?

Janine: Sorry, I don't. I like you but I'm not ready yet. We can still have a good time without having sex. Is that cool?

Doug: If that's what you want.

Janine: What do you want?

Doug: I just want to be with you . . . in any way I can. We can wait.

(Written for the Teen Alert Program, Domestic Violence Clearinghouse and Legal Hotline, Honolulu. Used by permission of Daryl Bonilla.)

Students are asked by members of Teen Alert to volunteer to play characters in both the skit where the male uses manipulative tactics to coerce his girlfriend into having sex, and in "We Can Wait." The response has been very positive. "We do the companion piece first, followed by 'We Can Wait' and then talk about both skits together," Daryl explains. "We ask the kids to tell us what they found healthy and unhealthy in the scenarios. We find that the visual aspects of the skits really help the kids to identify red flags in the first scene. And they respond very positively to how the girl and guy are respectful toward each other in 'We Can Wait.'"

Healthy modeling through esteem building: Erica Staab Westmoreland

I've found that teens get really excited when adults are truly interested in them. They are like human lie detectors, amazingly adept at picking up on who genuinely cares about what matters to them.

I try to be a good example for teens in both my personal and professional life. I let them know I remember what it was like to be their age. But my focus is always on them, not on me. I also make sure that I compliment each teen as the unique individual they are. Because teenagers are so concerned about their physical appearance, I'll often say such things as, "You have the most beautiful smile. You light up the room when you walk in."

When I talk with teens about sexuality, I don't focus on their physical appearance, but on the way they carry themselves. I also make sure they realize they're in charge of their own bodies. "This is your precious body," I say to them; "You get to say who enters into your space emotionally, physically, sexually." I impress upon teens the power and responsibility there is in having choices. Others must respect the boundaries they set, I say; and they themselves need to make decisions that are healthy for their own lives.

Healthy modeling, peer to peer: Alternatives to Domestic Violence (ADV)

The Teen Violence Prevention Program was developed to provide education and outreach services to middle and high school students in the Corona/Norco Unified School District of Southern California. The Coalition for Family Preservation (a program funded by ADV) collaborators includes Alternatives to Domestic Violence, Riverside County Public Health Department, Corona/Norco Unified School District, and U.N.I.T.Y. (United Neighbors Involving Today's Youth). Since its beginning in 1997, the Coalition has provided classroom presentations; peer counseling education and training; follow-up crisis assessment counseling; advocacy; on-campus support groups; TEEN TALK Youth Summits; and community referrals for teens dealing with domestic violence, anger problems, and other issues associated with violence. The program has reached over twenty-five thousand students in this school district.

The program objectives include:

- Increasing awareness of abuse and violence by helping students foster self-esteem and respect for themselves and peers through healthy and positive interactions.
- Increasing the number of middle and high school students who seek information, intervention, or counseling to assist in the elimination of dating and other forms of teen violence.
- Providing training and mentoring to high school peer counselors with the goal of using these students on campus and in the community to co-partner through peer-to-peer education about the issues of teen dating violence prevention.
- Developing and providing an innovative curriculum for middle and high school education that addresses violence that teens might experience. Topics include: dating violence prevention, establishing healthy relationships, anti-bullying and conflict resolution skills, and strategies for anger management.

Gina Graham Palmer has worked with Alternatives to Domestic Violence for the past nine years. She is a family violence prevention specialist, and is also responsible for the Teen Violence Prevention Program. "Teenagers will often times go to one another to discuss their problems,"Ms. Palmer says, "so we at ADV decided it would be in our and their best interests to go into peer counseling classes throughout the district on the high school level. Because so many students will become involved in dangerous dating relationships, we wanted them to have the awareness, knowledge, information, and the facts so that when another teen comes to them, peer counselors would know how to appropriately deal with their situation."

Peer counselors receive five days of intense training from ADV's Teen Violence Prevention Specialists. The youth are introduced to the tactics perpetrators use; receive data on prevention; develop a list of safe dating suggestions; learn peer counseling techniques for successful interactions; learn about the concepts of confidentiality, empathy, and objectivity; engage in creative role-play; and work on improving their active listening skills. On the final day, facilitators lead a large group discussion. Here, the students discuss the exercises they learned during the training.

More than one hundred students take ADV's peer counselor training each year. Ms. Palmer has a special wish for each of them. "I want the teens to eventually become community educators on dating violence prevention and intervention strategies in their own right," she says.

Healthy Modeling through Faith: How Christian Leaders and Lay People Can Help

For more than twenty years, Dr. L. Kevin Hamberger has worked as clinical psychologist on the faculty of the Medical College of Wisconsin Family Practice Residency Program in Racine, Wisconsin. During the first fifteen years of his career, Dr. Hamberger focused primarily on conducting treatment and research with men who batter their wives and girlfriends. For the past five years, he has been spending more time providing therapy for victims-survivors of domestic violence.

Dr. Hamberger is also a longtime Christian. For the last three years, he has taught a Sunday school class for seventh and eighth graders at his church. "There are many, many great opportunities to integrate nonviolent issues into youth Bible stories," Dr. Hamberger says. "Stories of God's grace, stories of faith, and stories of respect, including respect for one's intimate partner, are lifted up throughout Scripture. I use these stories as opportunities to discuss with Christian teens how they need to live their lives."

Dr. Hamberger is clear with the youth in his class about the importance of nonviolence in all aspects of their lives.

"I tell the adolescents that abuse can never be part of their relationship," he says. "I remind them that Scripture informs us about the importance of treating each other with dignity, equality, respect, and value. I think the church becomes an impediment to healthy dating relationships and healthy marriages when we let go unchallenged the notion that males have more power and value than do females. This makes it much easier for a male to justify abuse of his female intimate partner. We are to treat all of our human relationships as we experience the grace of God in God's relationship with us."

Positive Mentoring: Pastor Rick Roberts

"I think the most effective way to help teens form healthy relationships is to make sure they have positive adult mentors," says Rick Roberts, pastor of children and family ministries at Kenosha Bible Church. "I am referring not only to parents, but also relationships with other trusted adults in the context of church programs. These relationships need to go deeper than making sure that teens know their Bible verses. I'm speaking of relationships where kids can see Jesus Christ lived out in the way that an adult conducts herself or himself at church, home, and in the community. Many teens are reluctant to share difficult topics with their own parents. An adult mentor can provide the guidance and wisdom to help teens avoid those relationships that are not healthy for them."

Modeling from the Pulpit

Sermons on the qualities that make a dating relationship healthy between Christian youth are essential. If clergy and youth pastors choose not to address this issue from the pulpit, then Christian teens will turn to their peers and to popular culture for information. As we have seen throughout this book, these choices leave youth very susceptible to unhealthy situations.

These sermons must also state definitively that abuse and violence is always inexcusable and wrong. Pastors must make clear that this type of criminal and sinful behavior cannot be justified, and is, in fact, condemned by God, Jesus Christ, and Christian Scripture. A sample sermon on qualities of a healthy Christian marriage is located in Appendix A. A word of caution: Prior to speaking on this subject, pastors need to familiarize themselves with the resources available in their community on teen dating violence and adult intimate partner abuse. Addressing these problems from the pulpit will surely bring victims and survivors to disclose their stories. This is an important step, and pastors need to make sure they are equipped to lead these individuals to the appropriate people and places.

Why Teamwork Is Essential

> The main message I want to give parents and pastors, I think, is for them to be open to what teens are saying. And if adults don't know how to either deal with what a teen is telling them or it's too much for them to handle, please seek the resources in their communities.
> —Stephanie Liester, co-clinical director of therapy service, Safe Nest, Las Vegas, Nevada

A fourteen-year-old girl, who we'll call Nancy, came rushing toward me from near the back of the crowded sanctuary. I'd just concluded a two-hour workshop with Christian youth, parents, and pastors on teen dating violence awareness. Nancy, I soon learned, wanted to tell me about her best friend, another fourteen-year-old girl—let's call her "Kim."

"Pastor Al," Nancy said as her voice quivered uncontrollably, "my best friend, Kim, thinks she might be pregnant after her boyfriend forced her to have sex. She's really scared. We went to my mom for help, but all she said was 'Kim, as a Christian, you shouldn't have been having sex in the first place.' Mom then turned her back and walked away. Kim and I then told our youth pastor what had happened. All he did was tell Kim and me that sex before marriage is a sin. He didn't offer us any prayers, didn't recite any comforting Bible verses, and he didn't even ask Kim how she was feeling. Neither the youth pastor nor my mom said anything about Kim's boyfriend forcing her to have sex. They just wanted to judge her."

The above story illustrates why it is essential for parents and pastors to work as members of a larger team of citizens concerned with ending violence in teen dating relationships. As Nancy's disclosure vividly reveals, her mother and youth pastor judged Kim for sexual activity forced upon her, rather than concentrating on the critical issue—getting Kim the help she needed after her boyfriend raped her. Teamwork between members of the Christian church and community service providers make this type of miscalculated response far less likely. Partnerships also help victims and survivors receive more comprehensive care and services, and assist in holding perpetrators accountable for their crimes and sins. For example, had Nancy's mother and youth pastor worked as a team with community service providers, the police would have likely arrested the young man who raped Kim.

Christian youth who are violated emotionally, physically, sexually, and spiritually by a dating partner often need assistance from a broad scope of professionals and volunteers: advocates, child protective services providers, crises intervention counselors, law enforcement officers, legal professionals, sexual assault counselors, shelter workers, and victim and witness assistance personnel, to name just a few.[7] And those teens who perpetrate dating violence require assistance from offender-specific programs. This is a far greater task than parents and pastors can handle alone. Not all services offered to cohabitating partners or married couples are available to teens in an abusive dating relationship. Parents and pastors need to check with their state coalitions to learn about specific services for teens in their area.

The bottom line is that Christian leaders, laity, and community service providers need each other. None of us is qualified to handle alone all the complexities associated with teen dating violence. And when we try to work without the benefit of one another, we often end up compromising the safety and security of those adolescent girls and boys who desperately need our support. Teamwork is an essential component in ending the abuse and violence that is destroying the lives of so many of our daughters and sons.

Conclusion

Healthy dating relationships between teens are never guaranteed, not even when both partners are Christians who attend church and youth functions on a regular basis. However, equipping adolescents with a variety of positive models is a critical step in the right direction. Still, it's not enough for parents and pastors to simply tell their daughters and sons what a healthy relationship should look like; we must also demonstrate this in our own personal and professional lives. There can be no abuse or violence in our own relationships with our spouses, partners, friends, or co-workers. When unhealthy behavior is present, teens are likely to be turned off by our hypocrisy and to seek guidance from their peers and/or what they see in popular culture.

Parents, clergy, Christian educators, youth ministers, and youth workers must provide models of healthy dating relationships for youth that teach females and males equal power and value. Otherwise, there will be an imbalance in the dating relationship, causing one partner—historically, the male—to feel privileged and the other partner—historically, the female—to feel devalued. This male hierarchy makes it easier for males to perpetrate abuse and violence and feel justified by God, Jesus Christ, and the Christian Scripture.

Last, parents and pastors must work with service providers as a team. Our daughters and sons need the help of every member of the Christian church and the community if we are to bring an end to the abuse and violence plaguing so many teens today.

Questions for Discussion

1. What did you feel as you read about the ongoing struggles being experienced by teen-dating abuse survivors Amy, Angie, and Sarah? How would you, as parents and pastors, offer your support to them? Be specific.

2. As parents, what was your reaction to the reflections written by Curtiss Paul DeYoung and Shari Miller? What feelings and thoughts would go into a reflection you wrote for your own daughter or son?

3. What did you feel after reading the skit "We Can Wait"? How are you and your church dealing with the subject of teen sexuality? Be specific.

4. Are you addressing the subject of teen dating violence from the pulpit and in Sunday school classes? If yes, describe in detail the approach you are taking. If no, tell why you are not discussing this subject.

5. What are three dangers to parents, pastors, or a congregation in attempting to work alone with victims and survivors or perpetrators of teen dating violence?

6. As a result of reading this book, what are five actions you will take as parents, pastors, and congregation members to help end teen dating violence in your community?

Appendix A
Qualities of a Healthy Christian Marriage: A Sermon on Domestic Violence Awareness

What follows is a sample sermon I wrote for Teen Challenge International, Inc. It can also be found on their Web site, www.teenchallenge.com/index.cfm?domesticviolenceID =1&doc_id=333.

Although this particular message addresses qualities in a healthy Christian marriage, the principles apply also to healthy teen-dating relationships. Christian clergy, educators, youth ministers, and youth workers might use this sermon during October, which is National Domestic Violence Awareness month. It could be part of an entire month-long series focused on healthy Christian families. Topics addressed during this series could include: healthy parenting, healthy relationships among siblings, healthy teen dating relationships, and healthy Christian marriages. The sermon can also serve as a catalyst to assist Christian leaders as they preach and teach on the equal power and value God and Jesus Christ bestow on all humans, females and males alike. These teachings will help to lessen the undue privileges males have always been given by church and society. Before using the sermon, Christian leaders must first establish solid relationships with service providers within their community, so as to be prepared to deal appropriately with the survivors and perpetrators of domestic and family violence worshiping in their congregations.

Qualities of a Healthy Christian Marriage: A Sermon on Domestic Violence Awareness by the Rev. Al Miles

Let us pray. God, you are Love and Life-giver. We thank you for your grace, justice, and mercy. We firmly embrace your egalitarian nature. Through your son, Jesus Christ, all humans have the right to live life free from abuse and violence. May we treat one another with the same love and respect you give unconditionally. In Christ's name we pray. Amen.

Today we will address an issue that has unfortunately often been denied or overlooked by Christian leaders and laity: Abuse and violence within Christian marriages.

In Christian traditions, marriage between a woman and man is indeed a sacred covenant—an oath taken by two people before God and Christ, usually in the presence of family, friends, and other well-wishers, to stay together until parted by death. As part of most Christian wedding ceremonies, the couple also vows to honor, love, respect, and be faithful and kind to one another.

The author of a letter written to all Christian churches near the city of Ephesus (many scholars believe this person was the apostle Paul), comments on the holy and mysterious nature of this bond.

"Submit to one another out of reverence for Christ. Wives, submit to your husbands as to the Lord. For the husband is the head of the wife as Christ is the head of the church, his body, of which he is the Savior. Now as the church submits to Christ, so also wives should submit to their husbands in everything. Husbands, love your wives, just as Christ loved the church and gave himself up for her to make her holy, cleansing her by the washing with water through the word, and to present her to himself as a radiant church, without stain or wrinkle or any other blemish, but holy and blameless. In this same way, husbands ought to love their wives as their own bodies. He who loves his wife loves himself. After all, no one ever hated his own body, but he feeds and cares for it, just as Christ does the church—for we are members of his body. 'For this reason a man will leave his father and mother and be united to his wife, and the two will become one flesh.' This is a profound mystery—but I am talking about Christ and the church. However, each one of you also must love his wife as he loves himself, and the wife must respect her husband" (Eph. 5:21-33 NIV).[1]

Situations of domestic violence clearly stand outside of the epistle author's admonishments on the principles husbands and wives need to follow in a healthy Christian marriage. A married couple must love and respect each other, just as Christ loves the church. Domestic violence disregards these instructions and disrespects Christ and his church. Abuse is neither loving nor respectful. It is a crime.

As a "body of Christ," it is imperative that we gain knowledge on the many complexities associated with domestic violence. The problem involves a pattern of abusive behavior in which a person uses coercion, deception, harassment, humiliation, manipulation, and/or force to establish and maintain power and control over that person's intimate partner or former intimate partner. Perpetrators use economic, emotional, psychological, physical, sexual, spiritual, and/or verbal tactics to get their way.

We Christians must also grow in our understanding of who within an intimate partnership is most likely to be victimized and who is most likely to be the victimizer. While a small percentage of men are violated in both heterosexual and homosexual intimate partnerships, the American Medical

Association estimates that two million women in this country are assaulted by an intimate partner every year. The actual numbers are probably much higher because victims often do not report attacks, fearing both the stigma associated with abuse and the threat of reprisal from their perpetrators.[2]

Domestic violence is the number-one public health problem for women in the United States. According to the United States Surgeon General, domestic violence is the greatest single cause of injury among U.S. women, accounting for more emergency room visits than traffic accidents, muggings, and rape combined.[3]

These alarming statistics do not include many of the emotional, psychological, and spiritual tactics male perpetrators use to abuse their female victims.

It would require a great deal of naiveté on our part to think, given the overwhelming figures just cited, that Christians are somehow spared the scourge of domestic violence. To put it bluntly, there are men who sit in the pews and speak from the pulpits of churches in every Christian denomination and faith group who also beat, curse, rape, and in many other ways violate their wives and girlfriends. And there are Christian women and their children who live not in God's peace, but under the constant terror of being tortured emotionally, physically, psychologically, and sexually by males calling themselves "men of God." Some of these men are ordained Christian clergy.

Tragically, clergy and congregants have also misinterpreted and mistranslated holy texts and doctrine to support male dominance and female subjugation. The practice continues to this day.

The patriarchal system has certainly always been alive and well in Christianity. Both the Hebrew Bible and Christian Scriptures have an androcentric, or male-centered, perspective and emerge from patriarchal societies. Some texts, which are misogynist (women-hating), are lifted up to the exclusion of other texts that clearly affirm mutual respect between the sexes. Still other texts have been twisted—inadvertently and intentionally—to suggest that our loving and merciful God and Jesus Christ for some reason grant males authority and privilege over females. Because of all the above, men have received special dispensation from Christian clergy and laity alike to do whatever they desire with their wives, girlfriends, daughters, and all other females, without any fear of accountability.[4]

One passage of Scripture that has been used frequently down through the centuries to justify man's abuse of woman is the text cited earlier—Ephesians 5:21-33. Read in its entirety, the passage offers clear guidelines regarding principles that must be followed by both Christian husbands and wives. Love and respect are the virtues that need to be at the center of every interaction.

But over the centuries, the instructions put forth in Ephesians 5 have been used to elevate the status of men and put women down. Seldom do Christian clergy or congregants discuss the fact that nine of the twelve verses carry instructions for Christian husbands to follow. An inordinate amount of attention has been paid to what these verses tell wives rather than what they demand of men. The passages clearly instruct husbands to love their wives as they do their own bodies. Nevertheless, the verses are often used to instruct women on what they are to do for their husbands—even husbands who abuse their wives.[5]

The manner in which some Christian clergy and laity have used Ephesians 5:21-33 is blasphemous. True blasphemy occurs when a teaching that was intended for good is distorted and misused to bring suffering and death.[6]

Let us take a closer look at what the author of Ephesians actually intended to communicate to first-century Christians about the qualities of a healthy marriage.

Verse 21 introduces a litany of instructions for household members. Called "the household code," these instructions on duties of household members are also found in Colossians 3:18-4:1. Bible scholar Andrew T. Lincoln observes:

> Typical of the content of all such discussions is the notion that the man is intended by nature to rule as husband, father, and master, and that failure to adhere to this proper hierarchy is detrimental not only to the household but also to the life of the state. Setting the household code within this tradition becomes significant for assessing its use within early Christianity. The tradition reveals that proper household management was regarded as a matter of crucial social and political concerns. Any upsetting of the household's traditional hierarchical order could be considered a potential threat to the order of society.[7]

Even though the household code reflects a common patriarchal social and political position held in ancient times, this truth remains: domestic violence is never condoned by Scripture.

Nevertheless, abusers, clergy members, and churchgoers have frequently misrepresented the concept of female submission to excuse men's violence and blame women for their own victimization. In fact, many of us who grew up in the Christian church were trained to think that the famous instructions to husbands and wives in Ephesians 5 begin and end with verse 22: "Wives, submit to your husbands as to the Lord." (NIV) Proclaimed by the clergy and other pastoral ministers from pulpits and at weddings, and by parents, teachers, and other congregants as well, Ephesians 5:22 has established a foundation on which countless numbers of Christian marriages have been built.[8]

The verse has also been a perfect setup for millions of women to suffer acts of domestic violence.[9]

Over the years, hundreds of violated Christian women have disclosed their stories of horror to me. They've shared how their Christian husbands have beaten, cursed, raped, and violated them in several other ways. Often, the women have said, the husbands justified their criminal and sinful behavior by citing Ephesians 5:22. It's a husband's right, the battered women are instructed, to do whatever he wants to his wife. And no matter the atrocity these husbands commit, Christian wives are told that they need to graciously submit to them in all things.

Sadly, some Christian clergy and laity also propagate this treacherous lie. Violated Christian women have been told that Ephesians 5:22 demands that they "stay, pray, obey, and everything will be okay." Because of this inappropriate teaching, many Christian women have suffered greater abuse from their Christian husbands. Some of the women have been murdered.

In truth, the admonitions in the book of Ephesians to Christian husbands and wives begin not at verse 22, but at verse 21: "Submit to one another out of reverence for Christ." Inclusion of this one sentence puts on a whole new light and brings clarity to the entire passage. No longer can Christians view marriage as a male hierarchical union. Instead, we are challenged to observe the covenant of matrimony like God and Christ intended: as a mutual and egalitarian bond.[10]

The Greek word *hupotasso*, which the New International Version of the Bible translates in Ephesians 5:21 as "to submit," also means "to align oneself with, to behave responsibly toward another, or to relate to one another in a meaningful way." Thus, the author of this book is instructing Christian husbands and wives to behave responsibly toward one another, align themselves and to relate to one another in a meaningful and respectful way.[11]

There must never be a hierarchical structure in Christian marriages. Even when husbands are both loving and respectful, when there is no abuse whatsoever in the nuptial, male headship and female submission work against wives because this type of union disallows a woman to be a full and equal partner with her husband. The hierarchical structure is ultimately disadvantageous for a husband as well, because it prevents him from reaping the benefits of sharing life with a woman who is equal to him in every way.[12]

Let us now move on to verses 23 and 24: "For the husband is the head of the wife as Christ is the head of the church, his body, of which he is the Savior. Now as the church submits to Christ, so also wives should submit to their husbands in everything."

What exactly did "headship" mean in early Christian thought? The Greek word *kephale,* often translated as "head," has a number of metaphorical uses in the Christian Scriptures. Ordinarily it denotes "source," "origin," or "preeminence," rather than "authority over" or "ruler."[13] Greek language scholar, Catherine Clark Kroeger, states in an article addressing the classical concept of "head" as "source": "To declare that man was the source of woman, that she was bone of his bone and flesh of his flesh, was to give woman a nature like man's own. She was no longer of the substance of the animals but of man. She was a fit partner, his glory and his image. 'Neither is the woman independent of the man nor the man of the woman in the Lord; for just as the woman is from the man, so man is from the woman, and all things are of God.'" (I Cor. 11:11, 12).[14]

What is clear, whether we are discussing first-century or twenty-first century Christianity is this: There is no justification for Christian husbands to abuse their wives in any way, at any time. Let me repeat: Husbands have no right—not by God, Jesus, Scripture, beliefs, teachings, or tradition—to abuse their wives in any way. Equality and mutuality in marriage also help Christian women to understand it is never their duty, responsibility, or lot in life to have to endure the illegal and sinful actions of their Christian husbands, whether these inappropriate actions are emotional, physical, psychological, sexual, or spiritual in nature. Domestic violence is always worthy of condemnation.[15]

The remaining verses, 25 through 33, focus primarily on a Christian husband's responsibility to his wife:

> Husbands, love your wives, just as Christ loved the church and gave himself up for her to make her holy, cleansing her by the washing with water through the word, and to present her to himself as a radiant church, without stain or wrinkle or any other blemish, but holy and blameless. In this same way, husbands ought to love their wives as their own bodies. He who loves his wife loves himself. After all, no one ever hated his own body, but he feeds and cares for it, just as Christ does the church—for we are members of his body. 'For this reason a man will leave his father and mother and be united to his wife, and the two will become one flesh.' This is a profound mystery—but I am talking about Christ and the church. However, each one of you also must love his wife as he loves himself, and the wife must respect her husband.

These verses clearly instruct husbands to love their wives as they do their own bodies, just as Christ loved the church. Christ never cursed, raped, or threatened harm upon the church in any emotional, psychological, physical, sexual, or spiritual manner. Husbands must follow Christ's example of self-sacrificing love.

Let's return for a moment to Colossians, chapter 3. Recall that much of what the writer of Ephesians has to say about the household code was adapted from this earlier work. In Colossians 3:19, we find a stern warning: "Husbands, love your wives and do not be harsh with them."

Domestic violence is harsh. This type of inappropriate behavior causes wives and children a great deal of harm and destroys marriages and families. I want to say a few words directly to husbands.

If you are in any way abusing your wives—emotionally, psychologically, physically, sexually, spiritually—know that your behavior is both sinful and reprehensible, and may be criminal. Please seek help for your problems from individuals who are trained specifically to work with men who perpetrate violence against their wives. See me at the end of today's service and I'll provide you more information about various programs in the area. I will also be happy to accompany you to these places.

In addition, I invite you to schedule weekly spiritual care sessions with me. During our times together we will pray and read passages from Scripture that teach equal value and dignity of husband and wife. We'll also discuss the larger theological dimensions of how God views men and women.

Please don't attempt to walk the long and bumpy road alone that can lead you to a healthy, violence-free life. I want to walk with you.

However, let me clearly state my limits: I will in no way accompany you further down the path you've already been traveling. In other words, I expect you to be honest with me—and to take full responsibility for the damage you've caused your wife and children. Blaming alcohol, children, pets, Satan, work, and your wife for the abuse you are perpetrating will inform me that you're not ready to tread the long and very difficult road that can lead to lasting change.

I hope you choose to get the help you need. The process can lead you to becoming the type of Christian husband God intends.

The qualities that make for a healthy Christian marriage today are the same ones addressed by the writer of Ephesians in ancient times. In order for a marriage to be sustained and grow, both husband and wife must commit to the biblical virtues of love and respect. They must also recognize that this love, which comes from God, binds them together as equals, rather than ordering them in a hierarchy. In addition, a wife and husband must behave responsibly toward one another, align themselves, and relate to one another in a meaningful and respectful way.

Last, we must acknowledge that a healthy Christian marriage has no place for abuse. Domestic violence is not of God; it destroys women and children. Christian clergy and laity must always condemn this behavior.

Let us pray. Loving God, in both ancient and modern times, there have been scores of Christian men, both clergy and laity, who have used you, Jesus Christ, the holy scriptures, and church doctrine to justify their criminal and sinful acts of violence against their wives. There have also been far too many non-abusive Christians who have chosen to remain silent, even after knowing of the destruction committed by so-called "men of God." We call upon your holy spirit to empower us to respond more faithfully to the needs of victimized Christian women and children, and to hold accountable those Christian men who perpetrate these heinous crimes. In Christ's name we pray. Amen.

Appendix B:
Selected Resources

Books

Adams, Carol J., and Marie M. Fortune, eds. *Violence Against Women and Children: A Christian Theological Sourcebook.* New York: Continuum, 1995.

Kivel, Paul. *Men's Work: How to Stop the Violence That Tears Our Lives Apart.* Center City, Minn.: Hazelden, 1992.

Levy, Barrie. *Dating Violence: Young Women in Danger.* Seattle: Seal Press, 1991.

Levy, Barrie, and Patricia Occhiuzzo Giggans. *What Parents Need To Know about Dating Violence.* Seattle: Seal Press, 1995.

Levy, Barrie. *In Love and in Danger: A Teen's Guide to Breaking Free of Abusive Relationships.* Seattle: Seal Press, 1998.

Lincoln, Andrew T. *The New Interpreter's Bible. Vol. XI: The Letter to the Colossians.* Nashville: Abingdon Press, 2000.

Miedzian, Myriam. *Boys Will Be Boys: Breaking the Link between Masculinity and Violence.* New York: Anchor Books, 1991.

Miles, Al. *Domestic Violence: What Every Pastor Needs to Know.* Minneapolis: Fortress Press, 2000.

Miles, Al. *Violence in Families: What Every Christian Needs to Know.* Minneapolis: Augsburg Books, 2002.

Murphy, Nancy A. *God's Reconciling Love: A Pastor's Handbook on Domestic Violence.* Seattle: FaithTrust Institute, 2003.

Murray, Jill. *But I Love Him: Protecting Your Teen Daughter from Controlling, Abusive Dating Relationships.* New York: HarperCollins, 2000.

Murray, Jill. *Destructive Relationships: A Guide to Changing the Unhealthy Relationships in Your Life.* San Diego: Jodere, 2002.

Murray, Jill. *But He's Never Hit Me: The Devastating Costs of Nonphysical Abuse to Girls and Women.* San Diego: Jodere, 2004.

Pipher, Mary. *Reviving Ophelia: Saving the Selves of Adolescent Girls.* New York: Ballentine Books, 1994.

Pollack, William S. *Real Boys' Voices.* New York: Random House, 2000.

West, Carolyn M., ed. *Violence in the Lives of Black Women: Battered, Black, and Blue.* New York: the Haworth Press, Inc., 2002.

West, Traci C. *Wounds of the Spirit: Black Women, Violence, and Resistance Ethics.* New York: New York University Press, 1999.

Curricula

Leah Aldridge, Cathy Friedman, Patricia Occhiuzzo Giggans. "In Touch with Teens: A Relationship Violence Prevention Curriculum for Youth Ages 12-19." Los Angeles Commission on Assault Against Women, 1995.

Ralph Fry, Susan Mejia Johnson, Pete Melendez, Dr. Roger Morgan, poems by Jim Jeffra. "Changing Destructive Adolescent Behavior." Rancho Cucamonga, California: Parent Project, Inc., 2002.

"Teen Talk Curriculum on Dating Violence, Bullying, Healthy Relationships, and Peer Educator Program." Riverside, California: Alternatives to Domestic Violence, 2002.

"In Search of Love: Dating Violence among Urban Youth." Philadelphia, Pa.: MEE Productions, Inc. 1995.

"This Is My Reality: The Price of Sex—An Inside Look at Black Urban Youth Sexuality and the Role of Media." Philadelphia, Pa.: MEE Productions, Inc. 2004.

Videos

Love—All That and More. A three-video series featuring teens talking with teens about healthy relationships. Designed to inform youth about the elements that make up healthy relationships and increase their awareness and understanding about abuse; it offers adults a window into the often private world of teens and seeks to motivate all viewers to seek relationships based on equality and mutual respect. Produced in 2001 by FaithTrust Institute in Seattle, Washington. (For more information phone FaithTrust at 206-634-1903; or visit their Web site at www.faithtrustinstitute.org).

In Search of Love: Dating Violence among Urban Youth. A MEE Productions Research Documentary produced in 1995. It is a companion educational video to the curriculum of the same name. (For more information phone MEE Productions at 1-877-MEE-PROD; or visit their Web site at www.meeproductions.com.

This Is My Reality: The Price of Sex—An Inside Look at Black Urban Youth Sexuality and the Role of Media. A MEE Productions documentary produced in 2004. It is a companion educational video to the curriculum of the same name. (For more information, phone MEE Productions toll free at 1-877-MEE-PROD, or visit their Web site at www.meeproductions.com.

Internet Resources

Key words: teen dating violence, teen sexual abuse, teen sexual assault.

These key word searches will lead you to many links to information, books, and organizations specializing in teen dating violence prevention and intervention.

Agencies and Organizations Cited in Book

Alternatives to Domestic Violence
P. O. Box 910
Riverside, CA 92502
Phone: 909-320-1370
Fax: 909-320-1381

Coalition for Family Preservation—Corona/Norco
525 South Corona Mall
Corona, CA 91719
Phone: 909-737-8410
Fax: 909-737-3517

Community Corrections Improvement Association
901 29th Ave. SW
Cedar Rapids, IA 52404
Phone: 319-398-3907
Web site: www.iowacbc.org/ccia

Dads and Daughters (DADs)
34 East Superior Street, Suite 200
Duluth, MN 55802
Phone: 888-824-DADS
E-mail: Info@dadsanddaughters.org
Web site: www.dadsanddaughters.org

Department of African-American Studies
University of Illinois at Chicago
601 South Morgan Street (M/C 069)
Chicago, IL 60607
Phone: 312-996-2952
Fax: 312-996-5799

Domestic Violence Clearinghouse and Legal Hotline
P.O. Box 3198
Honolulu, HI 96801-3198
Phone: 808-531-3771
Fax: 808-531-7228
Web site: www.stoptheviolence.org

FaithTrust Institute
2400 North 45th Street, Suite 10
Seattle, WA 98103
Phone: 206-634-1903
Fax: 206-634-0115
Web site: www.faithtrustinstitute.org

Hope Reformed Church
612 Ontario Avenue
Sheboygan, WI 53081
Phone: 920-452-5648

Institute on Domestic Violence in the African American
Community
University of Minnesota
School of Social Work, 209 Peters Hall
1404 Gortner Avenue
St. Paul, MN 55108-6142
Phone: 877-643-8222
Web site: www.dvinstitute.org

Kenosha Bible Church
5405 – 67th Street
Kenosha, WI 53142
Phone: 262-652-4507
Fax: 262-652-4344
Web site: www.kenoshabible.org

Los Angeles Commission on Assaults Against Women
605 W. Olympic Blvd., Suite 400
Los Angeles, CA 90015
Phone: 213-955-9090
Fax: 213-955-9093
Web site: www.lacaaw.org

Medical College of Wisconsin
Racine Family Practice Residency Program
1320 Wisconsin Avenue
P. O. Box 548
Racine, WI 53401-0548
Phone: 262-687-5600
Fax: 262-687-5395

MEE Productions, Inc.
340 North 12th Street, Suite 503
Philadelphia, PA 19107
Phone: 1-877-MEE-PROD
Fax: 215-829-4903
Web site: www.meeproductions.com

National Center for Victims of Crime
2000 M Street, NW Suite 480
Washington, DC 20036
Phone: 202-467-8700
Fax: 202-467-8701
E-mail: webmaster@ncvc.org
Web site: www.ncvc.org/dvrc

Rape and Domestic Abuse Center
401 East 8th Street, Suite 311
Sioux Falls, SD 57103
Phone: 605-339-0116
Web site: www.rdac.biz

Safe Nest
Temporary Assistance for Domestic Crisis
2915 West Charleston, Suite 12
Las Vegas, NV 89102
Phone: 702-877-0133
Fax: 702-877-0955

South Carolina Coalition Against Domestic Violence
and Sexual Assault
P. O. Box 7776
Columbia, SC 29202-7776
Phone: 803-256-2900
Fax: 803-256-1030
Web site: www.sccadvasa.org

Teen Challenge International
Web site: www.teenchallenge.com

Urban Think Tank Institute
P. O. Box 1476
New York, NY 10185-1476
E-mail: UrbanThinkTank@usa.net
Web site: www.urbanthinktank.org

West Court Street Church of God
2920 West Court Street
Flint, MI 48503
Phone: 810-238-2631
Web site: www.wcschog.org/default.asp

Women's Resources of Monroe County, Inc.
215 West Main Street
P. O. Box 645
Delaware Water Gap, PA 18327
Phone: 570-424-2093
Fax: 570-424-2094
E-mail: wrmc@justice.com
Web site: www.enter.net/~wrmc/

Notes

Chapter 1

1. Dating Violence Resource Center, "Teen Dating Violence Fact Sheet." Available on-line at www.ncvc.org/dvrc, accessed October 11, 2004.
2. The National Center for Victims of Crime, "Help For Teenage Victims of Crime: Teen Tools." Available on-line at www.ncvc.org, accessed March 10, 2005.
3. "Teen Dating Violence Fact Sheet." Available on-line at www.ncvc.org/dvrc, accessed October 11, 2004.

   a. "Children Now," Kaiser Permanente poll, December 1995.

   b. M. O'Keefe and L. Trester, "Victims of Dating Violence among High School Students," *Violence Against Women,* 4, no. 2 (1998): 195-223.

   c. Avery-Leaf and Cascardi, "Dating Violence Education," *Preventing Violence in Relationships,* (Washington, D.C.: American Psychological Association, 2002), 82.

   d. Remarks by Judge Richard Lee at "Love and Violence and Perpetrators," New York City Coalition for Women's Mental Health, January 1991.

   e. C. M. Rennison and S. Welchans, "BJS Special Report: Intimate Partner Violence," USDOJ-OJP, NCJ 178247, (2000).

   f. B. Levy, *Dating Violence,* (Seattle: Seal Press, 1991), 9.

   g. *Teen Dating Violence Resource Manual,* (Denver: National Coalition Against Domestic Violence, 1997), 17.

The author extends a big *mahalo* to Niki Christiansen, Rachel DeYoung, Jordan Goettsche, Stephanie Liester, Shari Miller, Jill Murray, K. Daniel O'Leary, Vanessa Silver, Chris Stumpff, Erica Staab Westmoreland, Amy Woods, Claire Woods, "Angie," and "Sarah" for their willingness to be interviewed for this chapter.

Chapter 2

1. Al Miles, *Violence in Families: What Every Christian Needs to Know* (Minneapolis: Augsburg Books, 2002), 52-53.
2. Meg Meeker, *Epidemic: How Teen Sex Is Killing Our Kids* (Washington, D.C.: LifeLine Press, 2002), 159-60.

The author extends a big *mahalo* to Daryl Bonilla, Grace Alvaro Caligtan, Niki Christiansen, Rachel DeYoung, Jordan Goettsche, Jill Murray, Rick Roberts, Vanessa Silver, Kim Taylor, Melissa Thielhelm, Erica Staab Westmoreland, Amy Woods, "Florence," and "Sarah" for their willingness to be interviewed for this chapter.

Chapter 3

1. Ivan J. Juzang, Pamela M. Weddington, *This Is My Reality: The Price of Sex—An Inside Look at Black Urban Youth Sexuality and the Role of Media* (Philadelphia, Pa.: MEE Productions Inc., 2004), 5-8.
2. Traci C. West, *Wounds of the Spirit: Black Women, Violence, and Resistance Ethics* (New York: New York University Press, 1999), 137-38.
3. Ibid., 139-40.
4. Al Miles, *Domestic Violence: What Every Pastor Needs to Know* (Minneapolis: Fortress Press, 2000), 32.
5. See Miles, *Violence in Families: What Every Christian Needs to Know*, 68-69.
6. See West, *Wounds of the Spirit*, 140-41.

The author extends a big *mahalo* to Leah Aldridge, Akijuwon Greene, Lisa Brito Greene, Beth Richie, Chic Smith, and Oliver Williams for their willingness to be interviewed for this chapter.

Chapter 4

1. Al Miles, "Domestic-Violence Intervention and Prevention: A Challenge for Male Christians," PRISM, May-June, 2004, 11.

The author extends a big *mahalo* to Leah Aldridge, Daryl Bonilla, Grace Alvaro Caligtan, Niki Christiansen, Lisa Brito Greene, Shari Miller, Jill Murray, Gina Graham Palmer, Rick Roberts, Vanessa Silver, Chris Stumpff, Melissa Thielhelm, Amy Woods, Claire Woods, and "Sarah" for their willingness to be interviewed for this chapter.

Chapter 5

1. Rebecca L. Collins, Marc N. Elliott, Sandra H. Berry, David E. Danouse, Dale Kunkel, Sarah B. Hunter, and Angela Miu, "Watching Sex on Television Predicts Adolescent Initiation of Sexual Behavior," *Pediatrics*, Vol. 114 No. 3, September 2004, pp. e280-e289.
2. *Love—All That and More*, 3-video series and curriculum on healthy relationships. (Seattle: FaithTrust Institute, 2001), p. 23 of accompanying curriculum.
3. Dads and Daughters home page. Available on-line at http://www.dadsanddaughters.org/aboutus/about_index.html, accessed September 22, 2004.
4. *Daughters: For Parents of Girls* (Minneapolis: Dads and Daughters, Volume 9 Number 5, September/October 2004), editorial page.
5. See *Daughters: For Parents of Girls*, "The Dangers of Dating Violence," by Rain Newcomb, Volume 7 Number 2, March/April 2002, 10-11.
6. Ibid., 11.
7. Al Miles, *Violence in Families: What Every Christian Needs to Know* (Minneapolis: Augsburg Books, 2002), 138.

The author extends a big *mahalo* to Daryl Bonilla, Curtiss Paul DeYoung, Jordan Goettsche, L. Kevin Hamberger, Stephanie Liester, Shari Miller, Jill Murray, Gina Graham Palmer, Kelly Ritzman, Rick Roberts, Melissa Thielhelm, Erica Staab Westmoreland, Amy Woods, "Angie," and "Sarah" for their willingness to be interviewed for this chapter.

Appendix A: Sample Sermon

1. The Holy Bible, New International Version, copyrighted ©1973, 1978, 1984 by International Bible Society. Used by permission of Zondervan Publishing House. All rights reserved.

2. American Medical Association, "Facts about Domestic Violence." Available on-line at www.ama.org/ama/pub/category/4867.html, accessed March 10, 2005.

3. Domestic Abuse Project of Delaware County, "Here are some things you should know about domestic violence . . ." Available on-line at www.libertynet.org/-dapdc/, accessed August 14, 2001.

4. Al Miles, *Violence in Families: What Every Christian Needs to Know* (Minneapolis, Augsburg Books, 2002), 52-53.

5. Ibid., 68-69.

6. Ibid., 11.

7. Andrew T. Lincoln, "The Letter to the Colossians," in *The New Interpreter's Bible*, Vol. XI, (Nashville: Abingdon, 2000), 653.

8. See Miles, *Violence in Families*, 71.

9. Ibid.

10. Ibid., 72.

11. Ibid., 73.

12. Ibid.

13. Catherine Clark Kroeger, "Let's Look Again at the Biblical Concept of Submission," in *Violence Against Women and Children*, eds. Carol J. Adams and Marie M. Fortune (New York: Continuum, 1995), 136.

14. Ibid.

15. See Miles, *Violence in Families*, 73.

"More than any other author I've read about teen dating violence, Rev. Miles captures the unique and challenging issues facing young people today. This book is a critically needed resource for parents to learn about how to identify and prevent teen dating violence and the role their faith plays in these efforts."

—Robin Runge, nationally-recognized attorney-advocate
on domestic violence and the law

"Ending Violence in Teen Dating Relationships is a must-read for Christian families. Readers will feel astounded by the realities of teens' experiences with violence as Al Miles respectfully tells their stories. As usual, Al Miles is forthright, directly taking on the challenge of dealing with controversial subjects. He writes in accessible language to clarify complex issues. This book is full of useful information for teens and for adults to share with teens. We can all make changes that Al Miles proposes to protect teens, communicating openly with them about their intimate relationships in the context of their religious faith."

—Barrie Levy, LCSW, Adj. Prof, UCLA, author, *In Love and In Danger* and *Dating Violence: Young Women in Danger*

"The reality of intimate violence is a life-threatening physical and social problem in our culture. Yet, we often don't recognize its prevalence in the dating lives of teenagers. Al Miles has created a straight-forward book to assist pastors, parents, and all who care about the young people in their lives to stop dating violence. Using a thorough social and theological analysis, Miles explores those dynamics in both church and culture that support teen violence and those actions that we can employ to stop it. This book, with its direct, no-nonsense style, is essential reading for ministers, youth workers, families, and members of congregations who seek the well-being and safety of today's youth."

—Christie Cozad Neuger, Ph.D., Professor of Pastoral Care and Pastoral Theology, United Theological Seminary of the Twin Cities

"An essential resource for parents and clergy on teen dating violence. Reverend Miles cuts through the denial using powerful stories from young people to show us what is happening in many teen relationships and how we can respond effectively. A powerful, eye-opening, and useful guide."

—Paul Kivel, author, *Men's Work: How To Stop the Violence That Tears Our Lives Apart*

Made in the USA